MAKING WORSHIP REAL

MAKING WORSHIP REAL

A Resource for Youth and Their Leaders

by Theological Expressions in Arts Ministry
T.E.A.M.

Aimee Wallis Buchanan
Bill Buchanan
Jodi B. Martin

Geneva Press
Louisville, Kentucky

Book design by Sharon Adams
Cover design by Pam Poll Graphic Design
Cover art: Photograph by Greg Schneider

First edition
Published by Geneva Press
Louisville, Kentucky

This book is printed on acid-free paper that meets the American National Standards Institute Z39.48 standard. ♾

PRINTED IN THE UNITED STATES OF AMERICA

01 02 03 04 05 06 07 08 09 10—10 9 8 7 6 5 4 3 2 1

Library of Congress Cataloging-in-Publication Data

Making worship real / by Theological Expressions in Arts Ministry, Aimee
Wallis Buchanan, Bill Buchanan, Jodi Martin.— 1st ed.
        p. cm.
    Includes bibliographical references.
    ISBN 0-664-50168-0 (alk. paper)
    1. Presbyterian Church (U.S.A.)—Liturgy. 2. Public worship—Presbyterian Church. 3. Christian education—Textbooks for youth—Presbyterian. 4. Reformed Church—Liturgy. 5. Public worship—Reformed Church. 6. Christian education—Textbooks for youth—Reformed. I. Buchanan, Aimee Wallis. II. Buchanan, Bill. III. Martin, Jodi. IV. Theological Expressions in Arts Ministry.

BX8969.5 M35 2001
264'.05137'0071—dc21   2001040405

CONTENTS

ACKNOWLEDGMENTS

We would like to thank Dr. Lucy Rose and Dr. Chuck Campbell of Columbia Theological Seminary. Their "Preaching and Worship" assignment served as the backbone for this book. Dr. Rose was a genius in recognizing gifts, encouraging creativity, and supporting risk-takers. We are blessed to have been influenced by her and are grateful for her life's work.

Thank you, Beth Watson and John Knox Ranch, for inviting T.E.A.M. to lead a retreat that was the catalyst for this book. Thanks to Joan and Joe Martin for their endless hospitality and generosity, for their energetic cheerleading, and for baby-sitting our kids. We are grateful. Thanks to Jim Wallis for his countless hours of free consulting advice and to Joanne Wallis for her constant support.

Thanks to all our funny, inspiring, wild and crazy PSCE (Presbyterian School of Christian Education) friends who help us to maintain theological integrity, think creatively, recreate energetically, and keep moving down God's path. Vicki, Shauna, Mary, Danny, Bubba, Joe B., John McCroskey, Croskeys, Lynn, the Motleys, Leanne, Carla, Michelle, Mark, John H., Paul O., Laura, Steve—the whole bunch of you, you are a breed apart!

Jodi thanks Joe B. for all his love and support. She also thanks her boys, Joseph and Benjamin, who always waited patiently for Mommy to stop writing so that they could have their turn on the computer.

Aimee and Bill thank God for their two precious children and God's way of including them in T.E.A.M.'s goals. From Taylor's encouraging smiles to Elli's liturgical dance recitals, we are blessed.

Introduction

How many times have we seen it? Worship is under way in our local congregation. We look around to see who is worshiping with us. Our eyes turn up to the balcony (or perhaps the back few rows) and there they are—our youth. Some are genuinely interested and easily participate in worship. Some have good intentions but find themselves desperately trying to stay focused and participate. Other youth are simply there because they know their friends will be there too. They enjoy being in community, even if they are annoyed by the expectations to "stay quiet and pay attention." Still others are there because their parents made them come. They sit slouched in the pew, gazing out the window and wondering why they are there at all.

So, what about this predicament? Why are young people not fully participating in the worship of our church? Plenty of blame could be assigned to all sides. It's the youth. It's the parents. It's the ministers. It's the whole church in general. It's society at large. This book is not about blaming people for the problem but about offering solutions to the problem.

Certainly part of the solution lies in education. Many young people today have not grown up going to church. Perhaps they have not been taught over a long period of time about the rituals and symbolic meanings of worship and experienced their relevance. Perhaps in our transient culture, they have experienced a myriad of worship styles and theologies. Therefore, it is crucial that we teach our young people about Reformed worship, the worship style and theology of the Presbyterian Church (U.S.A.). Youth can more readily participate in worship if they know what it is that we are doing in worship and why we do it. When people understand why something is done a certain way, they are more likely to consider its relevance to their own life and faith. We hope that, through this book, pastors, Christian educators, youth directors, youth advisors, and youth themselves can teach our young people, in engaging and exciting ways, the wonderful tradition of Reformed worship.

Another part of the solution lies in the issue of culture and language. Carlos Cordoza Orlandi, professor of a global missions class at Columbia Theological Seminary in Decatur, Georgia, gives us this mental picture:

> Imagine you are in the mission field and trying to talk to the native people. You have something really important that you want to say to them. Some of the people have learned to speak your language, but many have not. Only a select number, then, can understand your important message.
>
> Even further, if you truly want them *all* to hear and understand your important message, you must learn to speak *their* "mother tongue." Their mother tongue is the language in which they think. It is the language in which they feel. It is the language in which they live. If you really want them to understand your message, learn how to say it to them in their mother tongue.

A few years ago, we were leading a youth group through a study of worship that would eventually prepare them for their youth Sunday. We began to ask the youth about worship services that had been significant in their lives. The youth immediately talked about the worship services at the Montreat Youth Conference. They said that the worship at the youth conference was much more meaningful than the "boring" worship they experienced in their home church. We began to explore what really made the difference between the two. It was not the liturgy, because the orders of worship were the same. It was not the music, because the last conference they had attended even used the organ and hymns, as did their home church. It was not the length of the sermon. In fact, the preacher at the youth conference preached twice as long as their home church minister usually did. Finally, one youth said, "It's because I can understand what they are trying to say. They talk like I do."

In our diverse and pluralistic society, young people have their own culture. They speak their own language, their own "mother tongue." It is a culture and language that is more visual than verbal, more contemporary than classic, more interactive than passive, and more dynamic than static. The language of young people is about words, but it's also about how they interpret and interact with the world.

Thus, if young people are sitting in the pews, we must seek to speak their language as much as we expect them to speak the traditional language of the church. This does not mean that all our sermons and liturgy should be full of slang or that all worship leaders should give up their robes for the latest youth styles. However, it means that we must make efforts to understand where our youth live, the way they hear and process, and the way they express themselves.

If worship is to be real to young people, if it is to be relevant, then we must help them translate the meaning of worship into their own real language. By doing so, they will be able to understand the significance of the rituals, symbols, and orders of worship. We can do this through education, but also by providing opportunities for youth to worship in their own "mother tongue."

We hope that, through this book, youth and their leaders will find effective ways to educate young people about worship. In addition, we hope this resource will help youth lead and participate in worship using their own styles and discover ways in which they can participate in worship using their own authentic voice. Whether you are planning a worship experience specifically for a congregation of young people or for a local congregation in which young people are a part, this book will help you share the good news of the Gospel with youth and empower young people to express their faith through worship.

HOW TO USE THE BOOK

This book is designed to follow the basic flow of worship found in many of our congregations. We begin with an introductory chapter briefly recounting the history of worship found in Scripture and the Reformed family. The chapters that follow are dedicated to particular elements of worship. The chapters follow the order of worship typically found in most PC(USA) and Reformed congregations. Readers from other denominations are advised to review the table of contents and adjust their use of the book to fit the particulars of their own worship tradition. In addition, the book ends with three chapters concerning the role and use of music, Communion, and baptism in worship.

The book can be used in two different ways. First, the book is an educational tool. The activities in each chapter can be used in a study and discussion format. Some activities are specifically geared toward teaching and discussing a particular element of worship. Other activities are designed to help youth learn by experiencing the elements in new ways. The activities are often followed by opportunities to discuss the experience.

Second, the book is a worship-planning tool. Whether you are designing a worship service for a retreat, for a youth Sunday, or with the congregation, the activities in this book can help youth think creatively about worship within the Reformed tradition. Some activities are better suited for worship in a nontraditional environment, such as a fellowship hall or outdoors. Other activities could easily occur in the sanctuary. Still other activities simply provide a means of creative thinking that can help your group develop new ideas for worship.

Our hope is that young people and their leaders will use this book to make worship real in their own lives, in the life of their group, and in the life of the church. Through learning about worship in their own mother tongue and experiencing worship using their own cultural styles, young people will find that worship is relevant to and the central action of our faith.

T.E.A.M.

In 1992, a small group of graduate students attending the Presbyterian School of Christian Education (now Union/PSCE) gathered around a fireplace to share dreams. Each came from an artistic background: one music, one theater, and one dance. All three grew up in the church and felt a calling to ministry. All three wanted to answer that call as well as answer a call to respond, in some way, to their love for the arts. However, bringing together the two different worlds of art and church historically has not been an easy task. Through sharing, prayer, and the will to forge new trails, Theological Expressions in Arts Ministry (T.E.A.M.) was born.

T.E.A.M. has grown and developed into an incorporated ministry with a board of directors that includes three founders: Aimee Wallis Buchanan, Jodi Martin, and Bill Buchanan. From 1992 to 1996, at PSCE and Columbia Seminary, we received a strong base of Reformed theology, education theory, and proclamation instruction. In addition, we were blessed to have professors who would give us the room to explore how we might express our faith through the arts. T.E.A.M. began its work by primarily keynoting youth retreats and conferences at local churches and presbyteries, and then on the national level (at the Montreat Youth Conference). Later we began coordinating worship for large events such as the Presbyterian Peacemaking Conference and the international Presbyterian Youth Triennium, as well as conducting numerous consultations and workshops with churches, presbyteries, synods, and seminaries.

Our ministry is both simple and profound. We work with groups of young people, helping them explore the biblical text and directing them in their artistic proclamation of that text to their peers. Sometimes it takes the form of a dramatic portrayal of a passage. Perhaps it is a series of monologues by modern characters where the truth and relevance of a text comes to life. Maybe the Word is proclaimed through a dance or liturgical movement expressing God's grace in motion. Other times the result is a choral arrangement of a song, a multimedia visual presentation, or a simple poem. No matter what the final result might be, the focus remains the same—to use all our gifts of expression to explore and share God's Word faithfully.

In 1999, we articulated our theory of worship and the arts in our first book, *All That We Are: An Arts and Worship Workbook.* In this book, T.E.A.M. describes a vision of worship through the arts by implementing both an inductive and deductive process of exploring Scripture. These processes emphasize that art does not lead Scripture; Scripture inspires art. The processes lead the reader into a deeper understanding of the text and serve as a tool for the discovery of artistic expressions.

In 2000, T.E.A.M. took a bold step to further its ministry. Through a series of long-range planning sessions, we worked to prayerfully discern God's will for the future of our ministry. In that process we developed a mission statement: exploring, illuminating, and nurturing faith in Jesus Christ through the arts with young people. All of our work is described in this mission statement. In addition, we claim a vision—to direct a center where young people explore and share their faith through the arts. At this time, T.E.A.M. is hard at work to bring that vision to reality.

CHAPTER 1

A Brief History of Christian Worship

Worship is and has always been one of the most important means of defining Christian life. It is through our liturgy, music, preaching, and praising that we most often demonstrate to the world what we believe. Christians are called to live together as God's people on earth. This means we, as the community of faith, are called to live according to Christ so that the people of the world will know who God intends them to be and how they should live in relationship with God. Our central identifying act as Christians, then, is worship. Whenever two or more are gathered, we praise God that we are not alone and that together we can proclaim the coming of our Lord to all. Despite persecution, abuses of power, illiteracy, war, and changes in culture, nothing has ever destroyed or dismantled the basic order of worship that our first Christian sisters and brothers once used. This fact powerfully demonstrates that God's work is at hand whenever worship takes place.

In the beginning, Christianity was basically understood as another sect of Judaism. The difference was that the Jewish Christians believed the Messiah had come and all that God created was at hand. The people would observe the Sabbath and go to synagogue on the last day of the week. On the first day of the week they would go to someone's home for prayer, Scripture reading, and the Lord's Supper. Depending on the community, the Scripture readings might include the Jewish Torah, a Gospel story, or one of Paul's letters (Gonzalez 1984).

Eventually Christianity was considered a separate religion. However, to outsiders, Christians simply worshiped another god and held rituals like everyone else. It was only when a person decided to join this new religion that the truth of Christianity became apparent (White 1993). Christianity was not your typical religious scenario, where you paid your dues, made a sacrifice every once in a while, and then went on your way. In order for people to become Christians, their background would be checked, their intentions would be questioned for sincerity, and they would have to commit to worshiping only one God and belong to no other religious cults or organizations. If it was determined that a person was serious, he or she began a three-year process of education and study before becoming baptized (Gonzalez 1984).

The early Christians met frequently throughout the week primarily for reading the Word and prayer. Worship continued to be influenced by the Jewish Passover meal and the Gospel account of the Last Supper in the upper room (Maxwell 1949). Baptized Christians celebrated Communion each week and followed it with prayer and the "kiss of peace" (a ritual of greeting one another with a kiss in the name of Christ).

As the church grew, it became more important to establish churchwide beliefs or doctrine. The leaders of the church (called bishops) gathered together or wrote to one another to discuss these instructions or rules. During this time of development, Christians went through cycles of persecution depending on who was emperor. Often the emperor would use the Christians as a scapegoat for the disintegration of an empire. The emperor would proclaim that the Christians were angering the gods since they would not worship them. Christians were asked to renounce their faith and burn incense to the Roman gods. If they declined, they were martyred. The hope of the emperor was that the persecutions would weaken and destroy Christianity, because no one would want to be a part of this religion. Instead, the more Christians were persecuted, the more their numbers increased (Gonzalez 1984).

During this time, worship was becoming more defined and began to have a structure to its weekly service on the first day of the week. What we call Sunday was a working day for those in the labor force, and the service was held either early in the morning or late in the evening in someone's home. Worship included reading the Word and praying for the Christian community, as well as for those who were not yet converted. A psalm or hymn was often sung, and then those who were not yet baptized were dismissed for study. The bread and wine were offered, and the prayers of the people were said. The offering was gathered for the widows, orphans, and sick in the community. Everyone was dismissed with the kiss of peace (Gonzalez 1984).

In the third century (313), Constantine became emperor. Constantine believed that for the empire to thrive and remain unified all the people had to belong to one religion. He believed God was calling him to make Christianity that religion. Bishops were raised in status and became the officials over the churches in the cities. Constantine gave money for basilicas (churches) to be built and consecrated as holy places. Larger groups of people began to worship together in one place instead of in individual homes. Some bishops believed true worship could occur only in these holy places. Churches were built to honor the apostles or martyrs in places where they were thought to have lived or died. Selecting a location based on this criterion was seen as proof that a church was an authentic place of worship.

Once the service moved into the basilica, the order of worship was expanded. Constantine brought to the church all the pageantry of an emperor. Worship leaders began to wear aristocratic clothing. Incense was burned during the service. The liturgy became more complex. The baptismal service was extended in length and elaborated upon in ceremonial acts. The congregation's role began to shift from one of active participant to passive observer (Gonzalez 1984).

Although the basic structure remained the same, several components were added to give worship a whole new look and feel. One of the most noticeable additions was the musical (played or sung) introit/prelude and postlude. During the introit, the bishops and celebrants entered in a procession and prepared for worship. As the pageantry increased, the processional and recessionals became more elaborate. Choirs sang in place of the congregation during the entrances and exits.

After the introit, a kyrie (prayer for forgiveness) was sung responsively with the congregation. As the service progressed, Scripture was read from the Old Testament, Acts, or the Epistles. The congregation responded by singing. Next, with all the drama possible (lights and incense included), the Gospel book was brought in for the Gospel reading. A deacon read the Gospel in Latin, not the language of the people. The people responded with a Latin phrase (whether they understood it or not) that asked for God's mercy upon them. The congregation then said a litany of response led by a deacon. A bishop or priest delivered a sermon on a Gospel lesson. Those who were not yet baptized were dismissed and the offering was received. The kiss of peace was then shared and the Communion service began.

The Communion service was also expanded to include more prayers said by the celebrants and hymns sung by the choir. The Lord's Prayer was said and a blessing was given before the congregation received the Communion elements. The service ended with the prayers of thanksgiving, similar to our prayers for the people, and a deacon dismissed the congregation (Maxwell 1949).

Worship was also affected by the great increase in the church's population. This growth created a need for more priests and church leaders. In response, the church quickly trained many priests. Bishops wanted to ensure that the new priests were doing things in the correct way. The bishops of the major centers of worship began to discuss and eventually write down a liturgical form to be used in worship. They created an orthodox Christian calendar and order of worship during the fourth and fifth centuries (Bradshaw and Hoffman 1991).

During the medieval period, worship in the church became increasingly mysterious to the everyday folk who attended the services. Worship, known as mass, retained the liturgical order of the previous era, but the form became a dramatic presentation that people watched instead of participated in.

One reason worship developed this way was the church's understanding of sin. The church understood that all people are sinful because of Adam's original sin and fall from the grace of God. Baptism, it was believed, was necessary to erase sin and allowed people to enter heaven. The church's problem was what to do with those people who sinned even after they had been baptized. The church created a system of penance in which a person had to do certain acts in order to be forgiven of the sin. Individuals had to earn their way before being permitted to take Communion or to go to heaven.

The second reason was transubstantiation—the changing of normal bread and wine into the actual body and blood of Jesus Christ during Communion. Only someone who was cleansed of his or her sins was considered worthy to handle the elements. Plus, this person would have to be extremely careful not to drop any of the elements. Dropping even a crumb would have been considered an abomination of Jesus. Only the clergy were deemed virtuous and meticulous enough to lead worship or handle the Communion elements.

Because the people were considered unworthy, they were greatly separated from the activities of mass. The liturgy was said almost entirely in Latin, a language the average person did not understand. Bishops and clergy were the only ones who had access to the Bible, which was also written in Latin. The bishop or priest would whisper the prayers and other liturgies throughout the service. Christians no longer gathered daily to offer prayers for one another. Instead, reciting prayers was considered the job of the clergy.

The Communion table was located on the east wall of the church. The priest was to face the Communion table during mass, so the priest spoke with his back to the congregation. Communion was witnessed at every mass, but the congregation did not actually eat or drink anything. The great highlight of the worship service was when the priest or bishop would hold up the bread for all to see the miracle.

The people took Communion only at Christmas, Easter, and Pentecost. Because there was the chance a person might spill the wine from the cup, the people were not allowed to drink the wine. They received a wafer of bread placed on their tongue by the priest. At the end of the medieval period, Communion was received only at Easter. At this time, people were disconnected from the service of worship, which was once an integral part of Christians' lives.

During the next period in church history, the church became divided. For our purposes, we will focus on the Protestant Reformation. The Middle Ages saw a movement away from the centrality of the Church of Rome. As regional conflicts divided the church, the church's authority was divided. This division of authority opened the door for an examination of Christian liturgy.

Martin Luther is known for his objections to church doctrine. Luther objected to the understanding that one could be saved by doing godly work for the forgiveness of sins. His liturgy for Christian worship exemplified his point that all were saved by God's grace through faith (Bradshaw and Hoffman 1991). One of the greatest contributions of the reformers was to put worship back into the language of the people. Luther's service was written and spoken in German, the language of his people. The hymns that were written were based on Scripture and sung in German.

Luther removed all of the ceremonial extravagance and replaced it with a simplified, inclusive service. The service began with the singing of a scriptural hymn and a congregational response. The worship leader welcomed the congregation and then read an epistle. After the congregation sang another hymn, the Gospel lesson was read, and the congregation said the Apostles' Creed. A sermon based on the Gospel text was preached. Afterwards, the congregation said the Lord's Prayer. Then, the people took Communion and were dismissed with a blessing (Maxwell 1949). Luther and other reformers wanted to return to the weekly celebration of

Communion, but the people, who had not participated in this rite for centuries, were unwilling. They settled for celebrating it four times per year.

Later, other reformers continued to reestablish worship practices of the early church. The reformers emphasized the full participation of the congregation and omitted any ceremony that prevented the congregation's involvement. John Calvin was one of these reformers. One of the most noticeable elements in Calvin's liturgy is the addition of a confession and absolution of sins. Calvin believed that the confession of sins and absolution (or assurance of pardon) prepared one's heart to receive God's grace and to hear God's Word.

Calvin's order of worship began with the reading of Scripture, followed by the prayer of confession and absolution. The congregation would sing the Kyrie or Gloria in response. The worship leader said a prayer for illumination before reading the Gospel lesson. Central to the service was the reading and preaching of the Word. It was followed by the Communion service, which began with a collection of alms. The worship leader offered intercessory prayers, ending with everyone saying the Lord's Prayer. The congregation sang the Apostles' Creed while the worship leader prepared the elements for Communion. The worship leader said the words of institution, and the congregation received Communion. The service ended with a prayer and a blessing (Maxwell 1949). Calvin's liturgy is the closest model we have for the current Presbyterian order of worship.

During the Reformation, the worship order still resembled the structure of the Catholic Church, but new possibilities from the early Christian traditions returned when the members were allowed to participate once again. Daily prayer was endorsed, and people were encouraged to pray in their homes. The Reformation prompted the return to the understanding that the home could be a place of worship. Full participation of the congregation in worship was reinstituted—and expected.

With the Enlightenment came new ways of thinking that brought about changes in the purpose of worship. This was the age of science, when it was thought everything could be proven. Mystery was overruled by reason, and the sacraments became a minor part of worship. Baptism and Communion were practiced only because the Bible commanded it.

During this period, people gathered together to find ways to gain individual virtue. As the quest for virtue increased, the need to admit one's unworthiness to God became crucial. Confession was the only way one would be able to accept God's grace. Confession preceded the hearing of the Word in order to prepare the congregation to hear the Word. The preaching of the Word remained central to the service (Bradshaw and Hoffman 1991).

The missionary frontier style of worship dominated during the settling of the western United States. The purpose of worship was conversion. The service was structured differently; it began with prayer and praise music that created enthusiasm and excitement. The Scripture was read and then the preaching would begin. The preacher's message was usually one of repentance. The preacher encouraged and even pressured individuals to make a commitment with the hope that they would be led to a profession of faith and baptism (White 1993).

Today the Presbyterian Directory for Worship provides instruction on the order and form of Presbyterian worship. It states, "Christian worship joyfully ascribes all praise and honor, glory and power to the triune God" (*Book of Order* W-1.1001). Presbyterian worship is primarily based on Calvin's understanding and order of worship. The form of worship can be flexible, and creativity in how worship is conducted is encouraged. Congregational participation is central through singing, reading, praying, and participating in leadership.

Worship continues to be the central act of Christians. It is through worship that we praise God, receive forgiveness, hear the Word read and proclaimed, and receive guidance and blessings as we seek to live our faith in the world. We celebrate as God's Word is enacted through baptism and Communion. The work of a congregation is born in worship as it has been since the beginning of Christianity.

WORKS CITED

Bradshaw, Paul F. and Lawrence A. Hoffman, eds. 1991. *The Making of Jewish and Christian Worship.* London: University of Notre Dame Press.

Gonzalez, Justo L. 1984. *The Story of Christianity: Volume I.* San Francisco: Harper.

Maxwell, William D. 1949. *An Outline of Christian Worship: Its Development and Forms.* London: Oxford University Press.

White, James F. 1993. *A Brief History of Christian Worship.* Nashville: Abingdon Press.

CHAPTER 2

Call to Worship

Sometimes a worship service will begin with a musical prelude, a time for fellowship, a time for prayer, or a time to meditate on Scripture, or perhaps someone will read a list of announcements. These events are important because they prepare us for the task at hand.

The call to worship is the official beginning of worship. It's the starting line, while the activities that precede it are the warm-up. It focuses our attention on our mission and purpose: to gather in praise and worship of God.

Who does the calling? God does. Worship begins with God. It always has. The Lord's day (the Sabbath or day of worship) marked the beginning of creation—the day long ago when, according to the Scriptures, God said, "Let there be light." The Lord's day also is the day of the new creation—the day when Christ was resurrected. Thus, all begins with God. And by God's Word, we are called to worship.

So, we participate in worship not in the name of ourselves or our own purposes. We call one another to worship because God has done the initial calling. We call one another to worship because God has called us first. We do the calling, the speaking, or the singing, but it is God's Word that motivates us, and it is the Holy Spirit that compels us. Thus, often a call to worship is a scriptural quote.

Psalm 95:1 says, "O come, let us sing to the LORD; let us make a joyful noise to the rock of our salvation!" Psalm 34:3 says, "O magnify the LORD with me, and let us exalt [God's] name together." Psalm 100:2 says, "Worship the LORD with gladness." These and many other Scripture passages are often used as calls to worship.

The call to worship can take on many forms, but it is usually a community activity. If the community is responsible for calling its members to worship, then the call to worship should include all of the community in some way. The call might be a reading done by one leader followed by a congregational song or hymn. It might be a responsive reading by a leader and the congregation. It might be a song or hymn sung by a choir or the congregation. It might be done in liturgical movement or in some other activity that involves the whole congregation.

The call to worship proclaims that the focus for the time together is to worship God and that we should ready ourselves for the Spirit's movement in our midst. The call to worship is our stepping-off moment. It is the leap off the starting block, the initial opening of the theater curtain, or the first sentence of the paragraph. It is when we proclaim that God has called us and we are ready and willing to praise and worship with all of our hearts, minds, and strength.

ACTIVITIES

1. Web Crossing
(15–30 minutes, active game)

Supplies: Two tables (stood on end and stabilized), two poles or trees; string, yarn, or waxed dental floss

Preparation: Tie the string between the table legs, poles, or trees to make a spiderweb. The spiderweb should start at about one foot off the ground and can go as high as seven or eight feet. Make sure the number of holes in the web is the same or greater than the number of people in your group. The holes should vary in size.

Directions: Explain that what the group sees before them is a spiderweb. The object of the activity is to get everyone in the group from one side of the spiderweb to the other using the following rules:

1. You cannot touch the web.
2. Once a hole is used, it cannot be used again.
3. Everyone in the group must get from one side to the other.
4. The group must work together to complete the activity.

If you have a group member(s) who cannot participate in the activity for physical reasons or member(s) who refuse to participate, involve them in the activity by telling them they are official web advisors and invite them to give ideas to help the group complete the activity.

Discussion Questions: After you have finished the activity, discuss the following questions. To make the most out of this session, encourage the participants to talk not in generalities but in specifics. Encourage discussion about their real-life experiences.

1. How did the group work together?
2. What did the group do well? What could the group have done better?
3. What did it take to get everyone to the other side of the web?
4. How is going through the web like trying to get to worship?
5. What are the obstacles or challenges in getting to worship?
6. How is going through the web like responding to the call to worship God?

The web-crossing activity is adapted from the "Electric Fence" (p. 209) in *Quick Silver,* by Karl Rohnke and Steve Butler (see the Works Cited at the end of this book).

2. Invitations from God
(10 minutes, art)

Supplies: Construction paper or card stock, markers, scissors, crayons, glue, newsprint, other art supplies for making a collage (yarn, sequins, glitter pens, pieces of fabric, magazines, etc.)

Preparation: Collect and place construction paper and other art materials on a table. Write "Who, What, Where, When, Why" in a column on a piece of newsprint or on a chalkboard and display it in the room where you will be working.

Directions: Explain the purpose of a call to worship using the introduction found at the beginning of this chapter. Discuss the following questions with the group: Why does God call us to worship? Why do we come to worship? If God were to send us an invitation to worship, what would it say? Then, ask them to think of answers for the who, what, where, when, and why of worship. In other words, who does God call to worship? What is worship? Where do we worship? When do we worship? Why do we worship? Record their answers on the newsprint.

If you have a larger group, divide the participants into smaller groups and give each group a different age, Sunday school class, civic organization, etc. that they can think about as they answer the questions again. Ask the smaller groups to share their answers with the larger groups. Otherwise, discuss the different categories as a whole group. Discuss the following: What are the differences in the answers? How does God speak differently to a group of three- or four-year-olds as opposed to a group of senior citizens? What are the commonalities in the answers? How is it possible for so many different people to worship together as one group?

After the participants have shared their responses, invite them to make invitations to worship. If they are making invitations for their own group, ask the participants to trade invitations when they are done. If they are making invitations for different people in the church, make arrangements to have the invitations delivered by volunteers from your group.

If you can get access to a computer, a printer, and/or e-mail, ask the participants to design invitations on the computer. They can either print the invitations and deliver them or e-mail them. This technology can be especially fun for many youth who are experts when it comes to computers and e-mail.

3. The Scripture Calls
(15–20 minutes, discussion)

Supplies: Bibles, paper, pencils

Preparation: On slips of paper, write Scripture verse references. Some suggestions are Psalms 124, 34, 100, or 95; Ruth 2:4; Romans 1:7; Luke 24:34; Romans 5:5; Isaiah 57:15; John 4:24; or 1 John 4:7–8.

Directions: After a brief explanation of the purpose of a call to worship, distribute Bibles and slips of paper on which you have written the Scripture verse references. This activity may be done in small groups or individually. Ask participants to find and read the passage. If you have divided the group into smaller groups, ask them to discuss the following questions in their smaller groups. If each individual has his or her own passage, you may discuss the different passages together as one large group or you may ask the participants to write the answers to these questions:

1. In your own words, what is the passage saying?
2. How is God or Jesus described?
3. What does God or Jesus say?

Next, ask the smaller groups or individuals to write a call to worship in their own words based on their Scripture passage. They may choose to write a chant, write or choose a song, do a responsive reading, create a poem, or do liturgical movement. Tell the participants that they can be as creative as they want to be. After everyone has finished, invite the participants to share their calls to worship.

For further discussion, you may examine the following questions:

1. How does a call to worship affect how you worship?
2. How does a call to worship affect the tone of the rest of a worship service?
3. How might we use the calls to worship we have created in other worship services that we participate in?

4. Called As You Are
(15 minutes, writing)

Supplies: Paper, markers, newsprint/chalkboard

Directions: In this activity, participants will consider the gifts God has given them and write a call to worship focusing on how God calls them to use their gifts to praise God. Before you begin, take a moment to remind the participants that they are each a child of God with different and unique gifts.

Invite the participants to choose a partner. Distribute the pens/pencils and paper. Each person should ask his or her partner, "Who are you?" ten times over. They should write down their partner's answers. After each person has interviewed his or her partner, ask the participants to write a call to worship for their partner. The call to worship should focus on how this person can use his or her gifts to praise God in a worship setting. How might that person give when it comes to preparing, leading, or participating in worship? For example, "You are my child. I have given you the gift of being a good friend. Come use your blessing of listening, smiling, and being hospitable to all the children of God. Come and worship me."

After the participants have finished, ask them to share quietly with their partners. Each partner should read the call he or she wrote for the other person. Another option is for each pair to stand before the whole group and read their calls to each other so that the whole group can hear them.

5. Life Collage
(20 minutes, art)

Supplies: Construction paper, markers, glue, scissors, paint, paint brushes, other art supplies for making collages

Preparation: Distribute art materials on tables.

Directions: A life collage is a picture that symbolically represents a person's life. It can reflect that person's spiritual journey or significant moments, steps, or phases in his or her life. A life collage is something that people can use to reflect on their life and share their stories with others. Once a life story is shared, it becomes a part of our collective story as a people of God. The significance of using a life collage as part of a call to worship is to emphasize that God calls each of us as we are. Worship is the place where we know we can come honestly before God and be accepted—no matter how wonderful, painful, mistake-filled, or glorious our life story might be.

Invite the group members to find a comfortable place to sit or lie. Ask them to take a moment to relax. Invite them to take in a few long, deep breaths and blow them out slowly. Ask them to clear their minds and focus on the questions you are about to ask. Ask them to think about these questions in a prayerful manner, asking for God's guidance and assistance as they think about their life. Then say, "Think back over your life. Start from your earliest memories. Think about significant moments in your life up to now. They can be moments directly related to your spirituality, like when you first began to understand God or when you were baptized. Or they can be other significant moments, like special times with your family, a certain birthday, hard times in your life, or rites of passage. Just let the significant moments bubble up in your mind." After giving the participants several minutes to meditate, ask them to open their eyes.

Explain to them that they are now going to have the opportunity to make a life collage. Invite participants to think of four or five significant moments that they would like to plot on a life collage. Invite them to choose a piece of construction paper. Using the art supplies, have each person design his or her own life collage. Ask the participants to try to stay away from words and use symbols, metaphors, colors, and texture to describe their lives. If participants need an example to get started, some helpful images are a road of life (using street signs and symbols to describe their life), a mountain range (with peaks, valleys, and rivers), or a weather map (with storms, warm and cold weather, droughts, rain, etc.). Tell the group members that they will be sharing their collage but will be asked to share only as much as they want to share.

If some members of the group seem to finish very quickly, ask them to go back and see what they might add to the collage. Ask them to be more specific or go into more depth. Some people may need extra encouragement; perhaps artistic activities intimidate them, or the whole activity might feel too personal at first.

After everyone has finished, gather the participants into small groups. Request that they share the highlights from their collage. If a person simply wants to show his or her collage and give no explanation, that is OK. After everyone has had a chance to share, read or paraphrase the introduction to this activity. Begin worship with a call to worship that you have chosen or written. As you read the call to worship, ask the participants to place their collages on a wall, the foot of a cross, or some other focal point for worship.

One option is to cut out squares of cloth to use instead of construction paper. The cloth can then be sewn together into a quilt or banner to be kept or used on more than one occasion. Another option is to cut strips of cloth for the collages. Participants could then weave their collage strips together as the call to worship is being read.

6. Roll Call
(5 minutes, game)

Preparation: Write down several different categories or topics that will identify the people in your group. You may also use some ideas from the following roll call list:

Eye color: blue, black, brown, green, gray, hazel, two different colors

Wearing socks, not wearing socks

Did/did not brush their teeth this morning

Slept two, four, six, or eight hours last night

Grade levels (junior or senior high, freshman, sophomore, junior, senior, etc.)

Play an instrument, sing

Sports: ride a bike, soccer, basketball, track, etc.

Directions: This activity is great for a call to worship because it demonstrates how unique and special we all are while we are still united as the children of God. Ask the participants to stand if the item you call out applies to them. Say, "Stand if you have brown eyes." All who have brown eyes should stand. Go through your list, instructing people to sit between each item you call out. End the roll call by saying the following: "Stand if you are a child of God. Stand if you are ready to worship God."

7. Shedding Old Skin
(10 minutes, art/discussion)

Supplies: Plain white masks, markers

Directions: When people come to worship, they bring all that they are to it, but they might worship more fully if they left some things at the door. Discuss the following with your group:

1. What kinds of masks do people often wear in order to hide who they really are?
2. What makes it possible for people to put down their masks?
3. What emotions, beliefs, or pressures (prejudice, pride, anger, etc.) prevent you from coming into a fulfilling relationship with God?

4. Do you wear a mask that hides who you really are?

5. What would happen if you got rid of that mask?

Distribute the masks and markers. Ask the participants to decorate the mask with pictures or symbols of the kind of mask they often wear. After everyone has finished, ask the participants to divide into pairs. Ask them to show their masks and explain the decorations. Remind the group that members can share as much or as little as they want.

Before entering the worship space, invite the group members to pray for the things they have discussed and thought about. As they pray, ask them to imagine shedding their masks like a snake sheds its skin. Ask them to imagine brushing off the layers of anger, resentment, pain, etc. as they pray. Leave these masks on the outside of the worship space or place them at the foot of a cross as part of the call to worship.

Another option is to change the metaphor. Sometimes the mask metaphor is overused and gets boring. Youth have "been there, done that." You may choose to use the metaphor of "baggage." Rephrase the discussion questions in terms of the extra baggage people carry around. You may further this metaphor by giving participants backpacks that are filled with rocks. Ask them to stand and wear the backpacks as they discuss the questions. Then, as they pray, they can remove the rocks one by one from one another's backpacks. They can remove the backpacks when they are ready to enter the worship space.

8. Call-to-Worship Tag
(10–20 minutes; large field or gym game)

Supplies: Boundary markers, bandanas, flag football flags or socks/pantyhose/strips of cloth to use as flags; some extra people to help in the game

Preparation: Designate outer boundaries and the worship space with cones, masking tape or other objects.

Directions: This activity emphasizes that, by joining together, people can praise God. The goal of this tag game is to get everyone to the worship space safely. The worship space should be in the center of the field or gym and should be outlined in cones or tape.

Designate a person or people to be "it" and give the individual(s) a funny name like the "Minister(s) of St. Mattress by the Springs." The other members of the group should wear flag football flags or tuck two socks/hose into their waistband at their sides.

The object of the game is for the runners to all get into the worship space before the "it" can take their flags. Runners can only enter the worship space in groups of two or more. Play begins when the leader says, "Go!" The young people run to make partners and groups to enter the worship space. Players can stay in the worship space for only twenty seconds before they have to run back out and help others get into the worship space. If the "it" steals a flag from a runner, the runner must return to the outer boundaries to get a new flag. Place the extra helpers around the field to watch boundaries, be timekeepers for the worship space, and give out new flags.

Once all the runners have gotten to the worship space safely, play ends. Play can also end if the "it" gets all the flags before anyone can get new ones.

Discussion Questions: After the game, discuss the following questions. To make the most of this session, encourage the participants to talk not in generalities but in specifics. Encourage discussion about their real-life experiences.

1. How did the group work together?
2. What did the group do well?
3. What could the group have done better?
4. What did it take to get everyone to the worship space?
5. How is playing the game like trying to get to worship on Sunday mornings?
6. What are the obstacles or challenges you face when you are going to worship?

9. Interview Your Neighbor
(10 minutes, discussion/writing)

Supplies: Copies of the interview questions and call-to-worship forms, pens/pencils

Preparation: Make enough copies of the interview questions and the call-to-worship form for each person in your group.

Directions: This activity is a process that will enable the young people to write personalized calls to worship for one another. Gather the group in a circle and ask them to count off by twos. Have the ones and twos join together to make pairs. Next, ask the ones to interview the twos for two minutes. They should ask as many of the interview questions as they can in the time allotted. Next ask the twos to interview the ones with the two-minute time limit. Encourage the interviewers to take notes, because they will use the information they gather later.

After the interviews are completed, ask the participants to write a call to worship for the person they interviewed based on the person's answers to the questions. After everyone has written a call to worship, collect them, mix them up, and pass them out to the group. Invite each person to read the call to worship they receive. Before starting the readings, remind the group to all say, "Praise God!" at the end of each call to worship.

10. God's Initiative, Our Initiative
(30 minutes, active game)

Supplies: One carpet square or rope circle (two or three feet in diameter) for each person in your group and one larger rope circle (eight feet in diameter) or four carpet squares put together. You may use tape to mark the large circle in the middle.

Preparation: Place the large circle in the center of the space where you will be meeting. Next, place the smaller rope circles or carpet squares around the large rope circle. The small circles should vary in distance from each other (between one, two, and three giant steps from each other). Leave at least three giant steps of space in a concentric circle around the large middle circle.

Interview Questions

What three adjectives best describe you?

What is your favorite thing to do?

What are you good at doing?

What is your biggest fault?

How would you describe this group?

How would you describe your relationship with God?

Call-to-Worship Form

Leader: _____ (name), God has called you by name.

You are _____, _____, and _____.

God has given you this group of people to _____.

Together, we will _____.

I want you, _____ (name), to come and worship.

All: Praise God!

Directions: The object of this game is for the group to work together in order to get everyone to the center worship space, otherwise known as "Planet PC(USA)" (or you can make up another name using your denomination's name).

Begin by asking for two volunteers to be "Temptation Aliens" who cause trouble for the rest of the group. Ask the other participants to stand on one of the smaller circles placed around the room ("asteroids"). Say the following: "The members of our group were on a space mission to Planet PC(USA) where we were going for a special time of worship and fun. While on the way, our ship was attacked by Temptation Aliens who did not want us to make it to worship or have any fun at all. We were all able to escape to our asteroids (where you are standing now). However, we need to get back to the spaceship" (point to the big circle in the middle of the space) "to complete our mission."

Now explain the following rules, which put restrictions on how the astronauts can move toward their spaceship, and explain the task of the Temptation Aliens.

Game Rules:
1. Your goal is to travel to the spaceship. Astronauts will want to connect with other astronauts in order to get there.
2. If you are alone on an asteroid, you can take only one step to another person and their asteroid. Your asteroid must remain where it is. You may not travel with it. Once you've taken your one step, you can take no more until you are joined with other astronauts.
3. If two astronauts join together, they make two steps and no more until they find more astronauts to join. They must also leave any asteroid they were standing on. They cannot take it with them.
4. If you find that you made a mistake in which way you stepped, you may take as many steps as you or your group is allowed to get to an asteroid and then start over (taking your allotted amount of steps in a different direction).
5. Once an asteroid is left vacant, a Temptation Alien can steal it. The Temptation Aliens can also distract, bother, and make communication difficult for all the astronauts by talking, "flying" in any direction, or getting in astronauts' way.

If your group somehow easily gets to the center, ask some of the group members to place the circles in new places of the room. Play again. This game will be different every time depending on where the circles are placed.

Discussion Questions: After the game is over, discuss the following questions. Remember: To make the most out of this session, encourage participants to talk not in generalities but in specifics from their own experiences and perspectives.
1. How did the group work together?
2. What did the group do well? What could the group have done better?
3. What did it take to get everyone to the spaceship?
4. How is playing this game like trying to get to worship on Sunday mornings?
5. What are the obstacles or challenges in getting to worship?
6. How is this game like the call to worship and our response?

11. A Moving Call to Worship
(15 minutes, liturgical movement)

Supplies: Cloth or paper streamers, a call to worship that you have written or chosen (a reading, a recording of a song, or a song to sing)

Directions: People can praise God in a variety of ways. One of these is liturgical movement or dance. Gather your group together, pass out streamers, and read the call to worship to them. Invite the group to create a liturgical movement piece to the call. Ask the participants to think of simple arm motions that could be done with the streamers as the call to worship is being read. The movements do not have to be solely waving the streamers, but also using them to make or shape a prop that represents a word or phrase in the reading. For example, a streamer might become a blanket, or several streamers put together might become a sun.

As the call to worship is read, played, or sung, invite the participants to do the movements they have created. As a preparation resource, it would be helpful to read the liturgical movement chapter in *All That We Are: An Arts and Worship Workbook.*

12. Movie Clip Calls
(45–60 minutes, discussion)

Supplies: TV/VCR, movie clips

Preparation: Gather a group of young people together to brainstorm a list of potential movie clips that would work for the purpose of studying or doing the call to worship. Then, preview their suggestions and choose several to use for the activity. Other movie suggestions are: *Grand Canyon; O Brother, Where Art Thou?; Jesus Christ Superstar; All the Pretty Horses; Mission: Impossible; Mr. Holland's Opus; Phenomenon; Dead Man Walking;* or *Hoosiers.*

Directions: Many movies contain powerful scenes of characters wrestling with God's calling, their faith, or how they can and should worship God. These clips can be used as an actual call to worship, or they can be used to study the significance of the call to worship in our liturgy. If you are using the movie clips as a call to worship, follow the clips with a call to worship taken from Scripture or one previously written by the group. If you are using the movie clips for study purposes, discuss the following questions.

Discussion Questions:

1. What clip did you like the best?
2. Who were the main characters in the clips?
3. What did they do in the scenes?
4. What did they have in common? What was different about them?
5. What is the message about God in the clips?
6. What clip seemed to most closely deal with the idea of being called to worship or being called to faith?

13. Basket Weave Prayer
(5 minutes, game)

Directions: Ask the group members to stand in a circle. Instruct everyone to raise both hands. Ask the participants to shake their right hand, and then ask them to shake their left hand. Now instruct participants to place their right hand in front of the stomach of the person on their right while still holding their left hand in the air. Make sure everyone is using the "correct" right hand. Next, instruct participants to place their left hand in front the stomach of the person on their left. Individuals should connect with a hand on their right and their left. Check for the following: 1. People do not have their arms crossed. 2. People are not holding the hand of their neighbor. (They should actually be holding the hand of their neighbor's neighbor.) 3. Participants have their left arm *over* an arm and their right arm *under* an arm (left-over, right-under).

After everyone is holding hands correctly, tell the group that they have made a circle with their arms and everyone is standing on the outside of the circle. Now invite them to slowly and gently, while still staying connected, raise their arms up and over one another's heads. Then they should slide their arms behind one another's backs. To do this successfully, participants will have to loosen their grip on one another's hands as they move. Tall people might have to bend over, especially if they are next to someone significantly shorter. However, once all the arms are behind all the backs, everyone should be able to stand comfortably in the circle while still holding hands.

Now tell the group members that they have moved from the outside of the circle to the inside of the circle of arms that goes around them. Explain how this is like God's family coming to worship. Everyone is called and everyone supports one another in the calling. Ask participants to think of one word that expresses their hope for or expectation of worship. Invite participants to share their words after you open the prayer. End by asking everyone to say, "Amen."

CHAPTER 3

Prayer of Adoration

After we hear God's call, we joyfully respond by entering into a time of worship. In God's presence, we are immediately struck with how great God is. We are inspired to praise God. The order of worship, then, is based on our response after coming into God's presence. We turn from the call to worship to a prayer of adoration. We respond to God's goodness by reflecting that goodness back to God through our action in worship.

A prayer of adoration is exactly what the name indicates—a time to adore God. Note that this is different from a prayer of thanksgiving, where we thank God for God's gifts and blessings in our lives. A prayer of adoration is a time to praise God for who God is. It is a prayer, not full of thanks for past actions, but full of descriptions of God's greatness. Usually, a prayer of adoration is full of adjectives that describe God or references to God's greatness as witnessed in the Bible.

The prayer of adoration is typically presented as a spoken prayer and is often followed by a hymn of praise. However, sometimes a prayer of adoration may take the form of liturgical movement, a series of praise songs sung by the congregation, the presentation of a banner, or a dramatic portrayal of God's goodness. The time of adoration most appropriately includes the congregation's participation, since we all are called to worship and praise God.

It sounds, then, as if the prayer of adoration is supposed to be the "feel good, sunshine and flowers" time of worship. What happens, though, if you enter worship and God's presence does not inspire happy, cheerful feelings in you? Does this mean you cannot participate in worship? No. Remember: Worship is an act; it is not a feeling. God's call for us to worship is not based on whether we feel like it or not. Even in the lowest times of our lives, we are called to worship God. The psalmist says in Psalm 69:2, "I sink in deep mire, where there is no foothold; I have come into deep waters, and the flood sweeps over me." Yet later in verse 30, the psalmist is able to reach into his faith and say, "I will praise the name of God with

24

a song; I will magnify him with thanksgiving." A prayer of adoration invokes a naming of God's greatness and faithfulness in good times and bad.

ACTIVITIES

1. Praise Marathon
(20 minutes, game)

Directions: Gather your group in a circle. Tell participants that they are getting ready to engage in a "praise marathon." The object of the game is to see how many times the group can go around the circle saying words or phrases of praise and adoration to God. Explain to the group that a characteristic of God is different from something God has done. This is not a time to focus on what God has done for us or given us but a time to focus on God's character. Who is God? How and why is God so great?

Give the group about a minute to think silently about characteristics of God. Then begin the praise marathon by saying, "God, hear our prayer of adoration. We praise you because you are . . ." Start with yourself and move to the left. Some examples are "loving," "caring," "forgiving," "a good listener," "supportive," "creative," "faithful," "offers hope," "freedom," and "powerful."

Please keep in mind that some youth in your group may have a wider vocabulary and a deeper knowledge of God than others. Give each group member a fair shot at thinking of something to say. If a person is still having trouble, open it up to the group to help him or her come up with a response.

If your group responds better to faster, more energetic activities, turn the "praise marathon" into a "praise race." Put a three-minute time limit on the game and see how many times participants can go around the circle.

Discussion Questions: If you are using this activity as an educational experience, use the following questions to discuss the activity. Remember: To make the most of this session, encourage participants to talk not in generalities but in specifics from their own experience and perspective.

1. What new things did you learn about God from doing this prayer?
2. Was there any characteristic of God that you didn't understand or that concerned you?
3. If you learn something new about God or learn a new way to praise God, how does that affect your relationship with God?
4. How does praising God affect your faith?
5. Why is it important (to God and to us) to have a prayer of adoration in worship?

2. Adoration Banner
(60–90 minutes, indoors, art)

Supplies: Bibles, a psalm of adoration, pens/pencils, paper, one large piece of muslin or one flat white sheet for each group, various pieces of fabric, glue or hot glue guns, scissors, paint and supplies for painting, fabric scraps, felt pieces, markers (permanent would be best), crayons, pastels, other banner-making materials that are available

Preparation: Place all the supplies in one central location so that groups can share them as they make their banners. Place banners around the room on top of drop cloths.

Choose several psalms of adoration. Some suggestions are 9, 24, 29, 33:1–12, 46, 47, 93, 96:1–7b, 96, 97, 98, 100, 103, 104:1–4, 113, 117, 145, 146, 148 ,149, or 150.

Directions: Divide your group into smaller groups of three to four members. Distribute the Bibles, pens/pencils, and paper among the groups and assign each group a psalm of adoration. Ask each group to read its psalm, and then ask the members to rewrite the psalm in their own words. After they have finished rewriting their psalm, ask the groups to design and make a banner that symbolizes their psalm.

After the youth have completed their banners, gather the groups together. Then ask each group to hold up its banner and read both the original psalm and the rewritten psalm. After each group shares, allow time for the participants to ask questions, make comments, and show their appreciation.

3. Group Cheers for God
(15 minutes, active game)

Directions: Divide your group into smaller groups of three to six people. Ask each group to think of a cheer that says something about God's greatness or praises God. It should be short and simple and have motions with it. When all groups have created their cheer for God, ask each group to first perform its cheer for the rest of the group and then teach the cheer to the other participants.

After all the groups have learned all the cheers, ask each group to huddle up and decide which cheer they want to do. Then ask all the groups to face the other groups. Tell the groups that on the count of three, participants should perform their chosen cheer. If it just so happens that two groups choose the same cheer, then have them join together to make one bigger group. Ask the groups to huddle up again to choose a cheer. Repeat the process until all the participants end up in one big group.

4. Alphabet Prayer of Adoration
(15 minutes, game)

Directions: Gather your group in a circle. Briefly discuss the concept of a prayer of adoration (highlighting points from the beginning of this chapter). In particular, point out that prayers of adoration center on characteristics of God more than on the actions of God.

Tell the group members that they will be working together to offer a prayer of adoration using the alphabet. Starting with yourself and, moving to the right, ask each person to name a characteristic or quality of God that begins with the corresponding letter of the alphabet. For instance, the first person might praise God for being "awesome," the next for being "benevolent," and so on.

At some points, participants are going to need help. How many characteristics of God start with "Q" or "X" anyway? Help the group keep things moving and keep the atmosphere light. Feel free to be flexible. For instance, "Q" could be "quite amazing" and "X" could be "eXcellent." The point is to help the group articulate how wonderful God is and why God should be praised.

Begin the prayer by saying, "O God, we praise and adore you because you are . . ." After you complete the sentence with your own response, remember to have the person on your right name a characteristic of God. Continue moving right. At the end of the alphabet, everyone should shout, "Amen!"

5. Prayer of Adoration Video
(60–90 minutes, art)

Supplies: Video camera, videotape, TV, markers, newsprint

Preparation: Make arrangements for access to a video camera and TV. If your group has more than sixteen people in it, you may want to acquire more than one camera. Make sure the cameras are charged, the tape is ready, and you have all the necessary wires to run the videotape on the TV.

Directions: Begin by reviewing the reasons for and concept of a prayer of adoration (highlighting points from the beginning of this chapter). Next, ask the group to brainstorm characteristics and qualities of God that could be included in a prayer of adoration. List the responses on the newsprint.

Next, divide the group into smaller groups of two to four people. Ask each group to choose a characteristic or quality of God that members would like to explore. Make sure there are no repeats between groups. Ask the groups to discuss the following:

1. Why is the characteristic important to you?
2. What does it say about God?
3. How could the characteristic be represented visually (through art, sculpture, drama)?
4. What things around us represent or symbolize the characteristic (trees, river, stained glass, etc.)?

Next, invite each group to design a video segment of a prayer-of-adoration video. Participants should plan the segment, including what they will tape, what action will be done, what voice-over will be done, and so forth. Some ideas are filming pictures of stained-glass windows in your sanctuary that symbolize the characteristic the group has chosen; making a group sculpture or creating a drama; or filming a scene outside. The video can be very concrete or take on a more abstract feeling. Encourage groups to be as creative as they want, keeping in mind that the goal is to clearly communicate the characteristic of God they are portraying.

All the groups should also practice taping the event by pretending they are actually taping. This is important, because unless you have access to editing equipment, each group will get one shot to get it right.

Put the groups in order and let each one have a turn to record. As they record, one group member should say, "O God, we praise you because you are _____." While one group is recording, the other groups can be working out the details for their section. At the end, record the whole group saying "Amen." Rewind the tape and play it for the whole group to see.

6. PowerPoint Prayer of Adoration
(60 minutes, art)

Supplies: Newsprint, markers, laptop with Microsoft PowerPoint or similar software, video projector and cables necessary to use it with the laptop

Preparation: Make arrangements to use a laptop with PowerPoint or another presentation program. If your group has more than sixteen people in it, you may want to acquire more than one laptop.

Enlist the help of a "computer expert"—someone in your group or church who has a lot of experience with this software. Ask that person to help you design a handout that includes the choices groups will need to make as they develop their slide (font, color, style, movement, clip art, music, voice-over, etc.).

Note: If you are not familiar with computers, this project may seem overwhelming, but your group probably includes several youth who think software is a "piece of cake." Find them and let them do the hard stuff!

Directions: To do this activity, follow the directions in the Prayer of Adoration Video (the previous activity). After the groups choose and discuss their characteristics of God, ask them to design a PowerPoint slide that represents it. The first slide of the presentation should read, "O God, we praise you because you are . . ." Next add each group's slide to the presentation. When the prayer is finished, add a final slide that reads, "Amen."

This activity is done most efficiently when one "computer expert" keys in the data and works with all the groups to inform them of their choices in creating a computer-generated slide (music, color, font, clip art, etc.).

Run the presentation on the laptop or through a video projector for the whole group to see.

7. Adoration Tunes
(20 minutes, game)

Supplies: Newsprint, markers, pens/pencils, paper

Preparation: Prepare a list of simple and familiar tunes (children's songs, church songs, choruses, or current pop hit songs). Some suggestions are "Mary Had a Little Lamb," "Jesus Loves Me," "Happy Birthday," "The Wheels on the Bus," "The Barney Song," the Doxology, "Row Your Boat," "The Itsy, Bitsy Spider," or the Gloria.

Directions: Begin by reviewing the reasons for and concept of a prayer of adoration (highlighting points from the beginning of this chapter). Next, ask the group to brainstorm characteristics and qualities of God that could be included in a prayer of adoration. List them on the newsprint.

Divide the group into smaller groups of four to six people. Distribute the pens/pencils and paper. Assign each group a different, simple tune and ask the groups to use the tune to create their own song of adoration. They can use the list on the newsprint to give them ideas. If time permits, ask the groups to make up motions for their songs. After all the groups have finished, have them share their songs with the entire group. If you have some particularly shy folks or "non-singers," the whole group can sing each song instead of each small group "performing" for the others. Provide newsprint or overhead sheets for the groups to write their lyrics.

8. Movement Prayer
(15 minutes, liturgical movement)

Supplies: A Bible, copies of the chosen Scripture

Preparation: Choose a psalm of adoration. Some suggestions are 9, 24, 29, 33:1–12, 46, 47, 93, 96:1–7b, 96, 97, 98, 100, 103, 104:1–4, 113, 117, 145, 146, 148, 149, or 150.

Directions: Gather your group in a circle. Ask a young person to read a Scripture passage to the group. Then ask the group members to turn and face the outside of the circle. Invite them to close their eyes. Tell them that you will slowly read the text again. Invite the participants to silently think about how they might express or symbolize each verse with their body.

Now ask the group to stand while still facing the outside of the circle. Read the text a third time. Invite participants, with their eyes still closed, to try the movements they thought of before. Remind them that they are not doing this as a performance for their peers but as a prayer between them and God.

Depending on your group's comfort level, you may ask the members of the group to turn around in their circle, open their eyes, and move to the passage as they face one another. Read the passage a fourth time as they move. You may, however, skip this step and move on.

Now ask them to find a partner. Give each pair a copy of the Scripture. Ask them to make up a liturgical movement piece by combining the movements they thought of as individuals. After a few minutes, read the passage again and ask all the pairs to move at the same time. Again, depending on your group's comfort level, invite the pairs to share their liturgical movement with one another.

You may determine that your group needs some other activities involving movement to "work up" to this activity. Several such activities are listed in our previous book, *All That We Are: An Arts and Worship Workbook*.

Discussion Questions: After you have finished the activity, discuss the following questions. To make the most out of this session, encourage the participants to talk not in generalities but in specifics.

1. What were you thinking and feeling during this activity?
2. How did you feel when you were praying and moving to the psalm facing away and with your eyes closed?
3. How did things change for you when you faced the group and prayed and moved to the psalm with your eyes open?
4. How did moving to the psalm help or hinder your understanding of who God is?
5. Why is it important to praise and adore God?
6. When is praising God easy and when is it hard? Why?

9. Prayer Journal
(30–60 minutes, art)

Supplies for journal making: Copy paper (for homemade journals), notebooks (any size works for store-bought journals), construction paper, glue, tape, scissors, stapler, embroidery thread, big needles, hole punch, yarn, crayons, markers, magazines, paint, stickers, and other art supplies for decorating the front of their journals

Supplies for prayer journal activity: Several newspapers; glue or glue sticks

Directions: Begin by reviewing the reasons for and concept of a prayer of adoration (highlighting points from the beginning of this chapter).

Invite the group to make prayer journals. If the group is making homemade journals, begin by taking sheets of copy paper and folding them in half. Then choose one piece of construction paper for the cover. Fold it in half and put the copy paper inside it. To secure the binding, staple it, sew it together using embroidery thread and thick needles, or tie it together by punching holes in the paper and threading the yarn through the holes.

If the group is using store-bought journals, the members will need to use construction paper to serve as a book cover for their journal. Most young people know how to make book covers from elementary school. If not, ask a teacher to show you how. If the journals are a larger size, ask the participants to choose a piece of construction paper to cover the front of their journal. Cut it to size and glue it on.

After the journals are made and/or covered, invite the participants to decorate the cover. The cover can be made according to a certain theme or a certain Scripture verse, or simply covered in the participant's own style and personality (representative of the youth, things they like, favorite Scripture verse, etc.). Remember: Creativity and not artistic skill is the key here.

After the participants have made their journals, ask them to browse the newspapers to find and cut out words, phrases, headlines, or pictures that could be used to express praise to God. For example, someone might use the words "joy" or "strong" or "helping those in need." Someone else might find a picture of a parent hugging a child or a scene in nature. Glue the clippings onto the pages of the journal.

Next, invite the participants to write their own prayer of adoration in their journal. Encourage them to keep in mind the clippings they have just used as they create their prayer.

After they are done, ask the group to gather in a circle. Invite individuals to share their clippings, their prayers, or both. Give time for the group to ask questions, make responses, and show appreciation for what is shared.

Another option is to try paper making with the newspaper clippings embedded into the paper. You may also mix in other materials from nature (flower petals, leaves, wood fibers) as signs of God's glory. Use the homemade paper as the journal pages or the front/back cover. Go to your local craft shop for simple kits and handbooks on paper making.

10. Adoration Collage
(60 minutes, art)

Supplies: Bibles, a variety of magazines (several for each person), glue, scissors, construction paper or poster board, pens

Directions: Introduce and explain the concept of a prayer of adoration using notes from the introduction of this chapter.

Distribute several magazines, a pair of scissors, glue, and a piece of paper (construction or poster) to each participant. Assign each person a Scripture passage. Some suggestions are Psalms 9, 24, 29, 33:1–12, 46, 47, 93, 96, 97, 98, 100, 103, 104:1–4, 113, 117, 145, 146, 148, 149, or 150.

Ask the participants to browse through the magazines and cut out words and pictures that describe the meaning of their passage. Invite them to arrange their clippings into a collage on the paper. Tell them to leave an empty space in the middle of the collage. Ask group members to write a prayer of adoration or words to their Scripture passage in the middle of their collage, using their clippings as inspiration.

Gather the group together in a circle. Invite individuals to share their Scripture passage, their collages, and their prayers. Allow time for the group to ask questions, make comments, and show appreciation for what is shared.

CHAPTER 4

Prayer of Confession and Assurance of Pardon

As we praise God for God's goodness, we are reminded of our own mistakes, inadequacies, and rejection of God's goodness. If we responded joyfully to the call to worship, then we respond penitentially to our praising of God. As we name God, define God, and bear witness to God, we are reminded of how far we fall short. However, as we think about our sinfulness, we are comforted by God's goodness and grace and, therefore, freed to admit our guilt and our sins. We come to God not in overwhelming fear but with the comfort of our faith. The prayer of confession is a time for us to turn back to God, confess our mistakes (sins), and ask God to make right what we have done wrong.

The prayer of confession is usually preceded by an invitation to pray, which includes a promise through Scripture that God will always forgive us. Most churches use a prayer of confession that the congregation reads together, in addition to providing a time for silent, personal confession. We stand to confess our sins together, because we are not solely isolated individuals who have turned against God. Being a Christian means being part of a larger community. The saving work of Christ is an action done for the corporate community. Thus, we gather together to confess our sins not only as individuals but as a community of faith.

The assurance of pardon immediately follows the prayer of confession. The assurance always reminds us that God is a gracious and forgiving God. We read Scripture or point to the life of Christ. We hear that Jesus died for our sins and reconciled us to God. It is as if the bridge between God and us was broken through our sins, but, through Jesus' life, death, and resurrection, the bridge has been rebuilt and nothing can destroy it again. The assurance of pardon reminds us that nothing—no sin, no mistake, no stunt—can separate us from the love of God.

The assurance of pardon is absolutely necessary, because, as worship leaders, we would not want to leave people wondering if they are forgiven or not. It is important to emphasize God's grace in the midst of our sins so that we may be freed to continue the worship and service of our Creator.

This ritual of confession and assurance in worship is a wonderful opportunity to get rid of our baggage, be honest with ourselves and God, and recommit ourselves to our faith journeys. It is not a time of judgment; it is a time of grace. It is not a time to fear God; it is a time to experience God's unending love through Jesus. It is a time to take a load off our shoulders so that we might more freely live.

ACTIVITIES

1. Case Studies
(30 minutes, discussion)

Supplies: Copies of the case studies and questions

Directions: Divide your group into three smaller groups. Give each group a case study. Invite the groups to read the story and answer the questions below the story. Allow about ten minutes for discussion. After the smaller groups are done, ask them to come back into the larger group. Invite the smaller groups to share a short synopsis of their story and to give their answers to the last two questions on the sheet. Invite the rest of the group to ask questions and make comments as each group shares.

For closure, ask the group to stand in a circle and join hands to pray. Tell them you will open the prayer with a time for silent confession. Then you will ask them to repeat after you a group prayer of confession. As the leader, open the prayer with, "Forgiving God, hear our silent and personal confessions to you." Allow about thirty seconds for silent prayer. Then say, "Repeat after me.

> We have turned away from you.
> We have even turned against you.
> We have not loved you, as we should.
> We have not loved ourselves, as we should.
> We have not loved our neighbor, as we should.
> We ask for your forgiveness. Amen."

Say to the group, "God is a forgiving God. Jesus has already reconciled us to God. Friends, believe the good news, we are forgiven. And all the people said, 'Amen.'" If the group gives a wimpy "Amen," get the group to repeat "Amen" until they shout it!

Case Study #1

Jim and Craig were good friends, so when school started they were glad to be in the same English class. Neither of them liked English, so it was fun to be with a friend. The teacher assigned the class to read *Romeo and Juliet.* Jim and Craig both thought the same thing: *boring.* Craig did not read a single page of the story. He didn't even bother with the Cliff Notes. Jim, however, decided to stick to it and read the whole thing. It was a good thing he did, because the teacher handed them a pop quiz on the day they were to have finished reading the play.

Jim was excited because he knew he could ace it. Craig knew he was in big trouble. He was already doing poorly in the class and this would surely get him grounded, probably even get his car taken away from him. As Jim filled out the multiple-choice answers on the page, Craig noticed he had a great view of Jim's test. He copied all the answers straight off Jim's page. Jim had no idea what Craig was doing. The teacher was suspicious the minute she saw that Craig had aced the test with the same grade Jim had. She called them to her desk after class was over.

She told them that she had given both of them "Fs" for cheating and that they were to go to the principal's office immediately where he would deal with them further. Jim was shocked and said there was no way he cheated. The teacher showed him Craig's paper with the same answers. Jim looked at Craig, waiting for him to admit what he had done, but Craig looked straight at the teacher and said, "Sorry, Ms. Jones, I guess we did it this time."

On the way to the office, Jim was furious. He told Craig he wasn't going to take up for him. Craig said he had to. Craig continued, "That's what friends are for. Besides, Jim, you don't want to look like a total loser and rat on me, right?"

1. What is the sin or sins in this story?
2. How would you feel if you were Jim? How would you feel if you were Craig?
3. What would you do if you were Jim? What would you do if you were Craig?
4. How is this action a move away from God?
5. How could Jim and Craig be restored as friends? How could they make their friendship okay again?
6. How could the relationship between Craig and God be made right again?
7. What would God say to Craig if Craig brought his sin to God?

Case Study #2

Helen was new in town. She was a bit different from everyone else. She dressed differently, talked differently, and basically did not fit in. Pretty soon most people in school didn't even want to be seen with her.

The Presbyterian church in town had a huge youth group and they always did lots of cool stuff. Youth fellowship on Sunday nights at the Presbyterian church was the place to be. Helen found out about the youth group and decided that maybe this could be a place where she could find some friends. She was very lonely and couldn't believe how bad the move to this new town had turned out to be.

Helen entered the church. When she walked into the youth room, all the noise and chatter stopped. Everyone turned and looked at her. There was silence. She felt like running out, but the youth director welcomed her to the group and asked her to come in. She sat down with a bunch of girls, but they did not talk to her. In fact, they snickered, giggled, and made jokes that she was certain were about her.

When it was time to eat, the youth made sure their table was filled so that Helen would have to go sit with the adults. When they were playing a game where everyone had to find a partner, the youth rushed to find partners with anyone but her. When youth fellowship was over, the young people all went to get some ice cream. They made plans to go right in front of her but didn't invite her. Throughout the night, the youth did nothing to welcome her. It was apparent that their attitude was to do everything they could to make sure she didn't come back. And Helen never came back.

1. What is the sin or sins in this story?
2. How would you feel if you were Helen? How would you feel if you were a part of the youth group? How would you feel if you were the youth director?
3. What would you do if you were Helen? What would you do if you were a part of the youth group? What would you do if you were the youth director?
4. How is this action a turning-away from God?
5. How could Helen, the youth group, and the youth director be restored as friends?
6. How could the relationship between the youth group and God be made right again?
7. What would God say to the youth group members if they brought their sin to God?

Case Study #3

Captain Walker was the captain of an oil tanker. His philosophy as a veteran of the oil tanker business was, "The faster, the better." After all, experience had taught him that the quicker you could get a ship to port, the more money you could make. He was known for taking chances like sailing in waters that were too rough or too shallow. He had made a good living, and his company was impressed with his record despite his many close calls with oil spills.

On this particular trip to port, Captain Walker's navigator told him they were headed straight for an area with sandbars and reefs. It would be next to impossible to travel through safely, so the navigator charted a course that would take them around the area. It would be much longer but much safer. Captain Walker was furious. He stated that caution was no way to make money. He demanded that the navigator chart a course straight through the dangerous area. The navigator did so, but unwillingly. As they made their way through the area, the ship hit a formation in the water and the boat leaked thousands of gallons of oil into the ocean.

There was great devastation to the marine life, many beaches along the coast were destroyed, land animals that live off the water were injured and killed, and the fishing industry suffered major losses.

1. What is the sin or sins in this story?
2. How would you feel if you were Captain Walker? How would you feel if you were the navigator? How would you feel if you were a victim of the devastation?
3. What would you do if you were Captain Walker? What would you do if you were the navigator? What would you do if you were a victim?
4. How is this action a move away from God?
5. How could Captain Walker, the navigator, and the victims be restored to a better relationship?
6. How could the relationship between Captain Walker and God be made right again?
7. What would God say to Captain Walker if he brought his sin to God?

2. Prayer Psalm
(15 minutes, writing)

Adapted from "Creating a Song Poem" and in T.E.A.M.'s *All That We Are: An Arts and Worship Workbook.*

Supplies: Copies of Psalm 51, pencils/pens

Directions: Tell the group you will be reading Psalm 51:1–12 to them. (Note: Psalm 51 is suggested here, but you may choose any psalm that has a repentance theme.) Ask the participants to listen closely to the words and imagine how the writer must have felt when he wrote this prayer. Ask the participants to close their eyes, sit comfortably, and listen.

Read the psalm slowly, giving time for the participants to think about the psalm. Read one verse, count silently and slowly to ten, and then read the next verse. End by saying "Amen" so that the participants will know you are done. Discuss with the group their responses to the following questions:

1. How do you think the writer felt?
2. What could have happened to inspire him to write these words?
3. What does the writer believe about God?

Now give each participant a copy of the psalm and a pencil/pen. Tell the group you are going to read the psalm slowly. As you read it, ask the youth to follow along, and circle any words or phrases that seem to strike them or jump out at them. Tell them to be choosy (you don't want them to circle the entire passage!). They should feel free to select five to ten words/phrases.

After you have read the psalm, ask the participants to make a list of the words and phrases they selected on the back of their paper. Then, ask them to write a prayer of confession by using each word or phrase in a sentence. By doing so, they will have created their own prayer or psalm.

Close the activity by opening the group in prayer and then giving people the opportunity to pray their prayers silently or out loud. After praying, say the following: "Who is in a position to condemn? Only Christ. And Christ lived for us, died for us, rose for us, and prays for us even today. Friends, you are forgiven. Believe it. Amen!"

3. Knots of Sin
(15 minutes, game/liturgical movement)

Supplies: Recreation hose or pieces of cloth that have some elasticity to them; a prayer of confession and assurance of pardon that you or the group have chosen or written

Directions: This activity requires a certain willingness on the behalf of the participants to be vulnerable (both in terms of physical touch and emotional expression). If you are using this activity as a part of a worship service, do the warm-up activity before worship begins. If you are using this activity as an educational piece or discussion starter, begin with the warm-up activity. It will be instructive in the discussion.

Warm-up activity: Gather the group in a circle. Ask the participants to hold their cloth in their right hand, extended into the middle of the circle. Then, ask the participants to reach in with their left hand and grab the end of somebody else's cloth/hose. Invite them to untangle the knot they have created while not letting go of their cloth/hose.

Confession activity: Ask the group to stand in a circle. Invite the youth to hold the cloth of the person next to them so that they make one circle connected by the cloth. You will need one volunteer to step out of the circle to be the "knot breaker."

Tell the group that you are going to read a prayer of confession. Ask the participants to think about what sin does to them as you read the confession. How does it make them feel? What are its consequences? What does it do to their relationships? Ask them to listen to the words while you read it through one time.

Tell the group that you are now going to read the confession again, but this time, invite the participants to, instead of just thinking, slowly move into a big entangled knot as you read the confession. Encourage them to do this silently and to let their movements reflect their thoughts and feelings about sin. They can form their knot by ensnaring and twisting one another and themselves.

After you have finished the confession, pause for a moment and ask them again to consider these questions briefly without moving: How does it feel to be entangled in sin? What are sin's consequences? What has it done to the group?

Tell the group members that as you read the assurance, the knot breaker will enter their knot and set them free. Tell them that when they are set free, they should form a connected circle again.

Begin reading while the knot breaker sets the participants free. After the group is back in a connected circle, you may invite participants to sing a song (the Gloria or some other song) or simply shout, "Amen!"

Discussion Questions: After you have finished the activity, discuss the following questions. To make the most out of this session, encourage the participants to talk not in generalities but in specifics. Discourage talking solely in hypotheticals. Encourage discussion about their real-life experiences.

1. What were you thinking and feeling during this activity?
2. How does sin make you feel?
3. What are the consequences of our sin?
4. What can sin do to a group like us?
5. In the first game, we got out of our knot ourselves. How is this like when we try to get out of sin ourselves?
6. In the prayer, the knot breaker got us untangled. How is this like when we bring our sin to God?
7. Why is confession necessary in worship?
8. Why is assurance necessary in worship?

4. Sin Twister
(20 minutes, game)

Supplies: The mat and spinner from the game Twister, or you may want to paint circles on king-size sheets and pin or sew them together.

Directions: This game is a humorous and fun way to be honest about all our sins and the trouble we can get ourselves into. Be careful that this game does not turn into a glorification of sin. Remember the object is to not get so twisted up that you fall down! Also, it is not necessary to play this game until only one winner remains. In Jesus, we are all winners. If any participants fall down, tell them they are forgiven and can start over.

Ask the youth to stand around the Twister mat. Tell them that you will name a sin and spin the dial. If they have committed the sin, they must follow your direction. Example: If you have ever lied to a friend (spin dial), place your left foot on green. Some other sample sins include

If you have ever lied to your parents . . .

If you have ever cheated on an exam . . .

If you have ever intentionally fouled in a sporting event . . .

If you have ever done something wrong and blamed it on someone else . . .

If you have ever called someone a name . . .

If you have ever called yourself a name . . .

If you have ever made fun of someone . . .

If you have ever made fun of yourself . . .

If you have ever tried to hide from God or hoped God wasn't looking . . .

If you have ever been disrespectful of someone else . . .

Participants may want to make a list themselves prior to playing the game. You may also limit the time line for the sins you select by saying, "in the past week" or "during today."

Be sure to conclude this game by reminding the group members that they are forgiven through the life, death, and resurrection of Jesus. You may also use the discussion questions from the "Knots of Sin" activity.

5. Throwing Sin Away
(10 minutes; works best outdoors; meditation)

Supplies: Rock(s)

Directions: As you invite the group members to confess their sins, tell them that you are going to pass around a rock. Tell them that sin is like a heavy rock. It weighs us down; it burdens us; it keeps us from being free—free to live as God would have us live.

Invite the participants to take a moment to feel the heaviness of the rock as it comes to them. What would it be like to carry that rock plus many more around with you all the time? What is it like to carry your sin around with you all the time?

Ask them to imagine placing whatever sin that binds them inside the rock as it is passed to them.

Begin passing the rock around silently or with instrumental music playing in the background. If you have a very large group, you will need to use more than one rock.

After the rock has come back to you, ask for a volunteer(s) to throw the rock(s) away as you say the assurance of pardon below. Instruct them to throw the rock(s) when you say that Jesus has thrown the rock away. The rock thrower(s) can throw the rock(s) over a cliff, into a lake or stream, or deep into the woods. The point is to throw the rock where it cannot be seen anymore. Conclude by everyone shouting "Amen!" or singing a song together.

Assurance of Pardon: Our sin is like a rock. It burdens us with its heavy weight. It makes it impossible for us to be who God intends us to be. But Jesus has forgiven us. He has set us free. Jesus has thrown the rock away. He lived so that we might learn. He died so that we might live. He rose so that we might believe! Friends, believe the good news! In Jesus' name, we are forgiven.

6. Sin Burning
(10 minutes; works best outdoors; meditation)

Supplies: Paper, pens/pencils, matches/lighter, a place to burn the paper (or a basket/trashcan to dispose of the paper if you choose not to burn it)

Directions: As you invite the group members to confess their sins, pass around paper and pens/pencils. Invite each participant to write a prayer of confession on his or her sheet of paper. Remind the youth that this prayer is between them and God and will not be read by anyone else. While they are writing, ask for silence or play some instrumental music in the background.

After everyone has finished, read Romans 8:38 aloud: "For I am convinced that neither death, nor life, nor angels, nor rulers, nor things present, nor things to come, nor powers, nor height, nor depth, nor anything else in all creation, will be able to separate us from the love of God in Christ Jesus our Lord." Remind the youth that there is nothing that they can do or be that will separate them from God, because Jesus makes separation impossible. Invite participants to wad up their paper and place it in the "burning area" or the basket.

As you burn the paper, say the following: "Jesus Christ gives us a new beginning. Our old life is gone so that we might begin something new. Friends, believe the good news. We are forgiven!"

As the paper continues to burn, invite the group to shout "Amen!" or sing together.

Option one: If you cannot burn the paper because of your location, you may throw the prayers in a trashcan or a basket. The basket could be placed at the base of a cross or carried out of sight by someone in the group.

Option two: If you are in a retreat/camp setting, you may want to have worship around a campfire. Thus, the participants could throw their prayers in the already burning fire, a metaphor for God's light in our lives.

Option three: If you are in a retreat/camp setting, you may use this activity to start a campfire. Worship would then continue around the burning fire as a celebration of God's light in our lives.

7. Spiral of Confession and Assurance
(10 minutes, liturgical movement)

Directions: Gather your group in a circle and ask everyone to hold hands. Invite the group into a time of confession by saying the following: "Often we find ourselves turning away from God. We do one thing after another that pulls us farther and farther away from our Creator. We often think we are getting away with it and can live without a Savior, but the truth is that we are really in a downward spiral that leads us nowhere. Sin does nothing but pull us down into despair, isolation, and helplessness." Invite the participants to follow your lead. As they walk, invite them to silently meditate on their sin and confess it in prayer to God. If you need something to encourage "silent meditation," try playing instrumental music in the background.

Break hands with the person to your left and begin to walk to the left around the inside of the circle. Do not let go of the hand of the person on your right. That person should follow you. As you walk, the circle should spiral around itself, getting smaller and smaller until you end up in one, tight bunch (you will be in the center). When you are in this position, say the following: "Our sin binds us and entangles us. But Jesus frees us and heals us. He lived so that we might learn. He died so that we might live. He rose so that we might believe! Friends, believe the good news! In Jesus' name, we are forgiven." Then ask the person who is the last person in the line on the outside of the circle (that person is the same person who was originally on your left) to begin walking in the opposite direction. That individual will pull everyone out of the spiral and back into one large circle.

As you walk out of the spiral, there are several options. Walk silently, inviting the group to pray silent prayers of thanksgiving for forgiveness, sing together, or listen to a song about forgiveness that you have chosen.

8. A Walk on the Dark Side
(30 minutes, game)

Supplies: Blindfolds, extra leaders to help with the walk

Directions: Give each participant in your group a blindfold. Ask the youth to stand in a line and place the blindfolds over their eyes. Say the following to your group: "Sin is a journey into darkness. It is our turning from the way of light to the way of darkness." Explain to the participants that they are now going to go on a blind walk. Ask them to silently reflect on the sin that keeps them in the darkness and away from the light of God. Ask the participants to place their hands on the shoulders of the person in front of them. You will hold the hand of the first person in line to go on the walk. Make sure the walk has challenges, but keep in mind the maturity and abilities of the individuals in your group. The extra leaders should silently walk next to the line to make sure the participants do not hurt themselves.

After the walk, say to the group, "Believing in Christ is a journey in the light. Jesus has forgiven us and brought us into the fullness of his presence. We are forgiven! Remove your blindfolds."

Discussion Questions: As a follow-up, you may discuss these questions. emember: To make the most out of this session, encourage the participants to talk not in generalities but in specifics.

1. What were you thinking and feeling during this activity?
2. How are those thoughts and feelings similar to what you think and feel when you are caught up in sin?
3. How did the blindfolds hinder you? How do sinful actions hinder you?
4. During the walk, we had the group and the extra leaders to help us; to whom have you reached out in the past for help when your journey of faith was especially hard?
5. How did those people help you?

Option one: You may do this activity as a "night hike." Do not blindfold the participants, but do not let them carry flashlights. Only the leader should carry a small light. You should still have plenty of helpers to ensure the group's safety.

Option two: Use this option after you have finished the group walk. Depending on the area in which you do this activity and on the ability of participants to maturely participate without being careless, invite each participant to walk alone and blindfolded from one point to another. Make the walk challenging and long enough so that participants have time to get a sense of what it is like to walk alone in darkness. You will need the extra leaders to prevent any falls. Allow only one or two people to go at a time for safety reasons. Use the following additional discussion questions:

1. How is walking alone in darkness like what happens with sin?
2. What was it like to watch the blindfolded person try to get from one point to another?
3. How did the blindfolded individual resemble a person caught in his or her sin?
4. How are the group walk and the individual walk different?
5. How are they the same?
6. Which one is more common to your experience of sin?

9. Confession and Assurance Banners
(45–60 minutes, art)

Supplies: Two sheets or large pieces of canvas to make banners (size is dependent on size of the group), several different colors of paints (tempera or acrylic), brushes, water, paper towels, drop cloths, cleanup supplies

Preparation: Place both sheets in the same space or room. Place them just far enough apart so that people can get around each sheet to paint. You may hang them on the wall or place them on the floor. Place drop cloths underneath them, because the paint will soak through. Arrange the paints, brushes, and supplies where they are accessible to both banners.

Directions: Gather the group around the banner on the left. Tell the group that you are going to enter into a time of prayer that will include silent prayer but also a time to pray through painting. Tell the group that the banner on the left will be the confession banner and the banner on the right will be the assurance banner. Explain that there are a couple of rules about making the banners. There should be no talking. The banner should not be a bunch of small pictures on the one big sheet but one large picture that the group creates by connecting their drawings together spontaneously. The participants should feel free to add to what someone else has done or connect their piece to another. The participants can write, draw, and so forth. There is no limitation to what they contribute to the banner itself as long as it stays within the theme. Remind them also that this activity is about expression and prayer, not about artistry. Someone who is not an artist has as much to contribute as the accomplished artists in your group.

As you invite the youth into a time of confession, ask them to close their eyes and think specifically of things they would like to bring in prayer before God. Maybe there are a series of things they need to pray about; maybe it is just one big thing they need to pray about. After a few moments of silence, ask them to think about the following questions. Silently count to ten between each question in order to give enough time for the participants to think.

1. How does your sin make you feel?
2. If you could give your sin a name, what would it be?
3. If you could give your sin a color, what would it be?
4. If your sin took form and shape, what would it look like?

After a few more moments of silence, invite the group to silently begin painting the banner. During this time, you may want to play some soft instrumental music in the background to encourage silence and to establish the appropriate mood.

After about ten to fifteen minutes, ask your group to put down the brushes and paint. Invite the participants to look at the banner that has been created. They may walk around it, sit beside it, or stand still to look at it. Invite them to continue in a time of confession. After a few moments, invite the group to gather around the assurance banner on the right.

Ask the participants to close their eyes and picture God before them. Say to the group, "Hear God speaking to you: Child of mine, you are forgiven. Who is in a position to condemn you? Only Jesus. And Jesus died for you. Jesus lived for you. Jesus prays for you right now. I forgive you. Find peace. Live in hope" (partially taken from Romans 8:34). While the participants still have their eyes closed, ask them to think about the following questions. Silently count to ten between each question in order to give enough time for the participants to think of a response.

1. What else is God saying to you?
2. How does it feel to be pardoned, to get a clean slate, to be freed from your sin?
3. If you could give assurance a name, what would it be?
4. If you could give assurance a color, what would it be?
5. If assurance took form and shape, what would it look like?

After a few moments of silence, invite the group to silently begin painting the banner. During this time, you may want to play some soft instrumental music in the background to encourage silence and to establish the appropriate mood. Choose music contrasting with that which you played during the confession.

After about ten to fifteen minutes, ask your group to put down the brushes and paint. Invite the participants to look at the banner that has been created. They may walk around it, sit beside it, or stand still to look at it. After a few moments, invite the group to gather in a place where they can look at both banners at the same time.

Discussion Questions: Invite them to discuss the following questions. You can use these questions either to enable a discussion or as a guide for journaling by the participants. After the discussion, remind the group once again that they are forgiven. Say the assurance of pardon (above) together or sing a song together to end the activity.

1. What were you thinking or feeling as you did this activity?
2. Which banner was easier to paint? Why?
3. What does the confession banner say about sin?
4. What does the assurance banner say about forgiveness?
5. If you were to give a title to this work of art, what would it be?
6. How are the two banners different? What are the outstanding and subtle differences between the two of them?
7. What have you learned about yourself from doing this?
8. What have you learned about God from participating in this activity?

10. Prayer Journals
(15–30 minutes, art)

Supplies: Copy paper (for homemade journals), notebooks (any size works for store-bought journals), construction paper, glue, tape, scissors, stapler, embroidery thread, big needles, hole punch, yarn, crayons, markers, magazines, paint, stickers, and other art supplies for decorating the front of their journals.

Directions: Your group can make prayer journals that can be used for one worship service alone, for one specific type of prayer (such as confession and assurance), or for many different prayers over a period of time. Use the prayer-journal directions found in the prayer-journal activity on pages 30–31.

CHAPTER 5

Reading of the Word

We have responded to God's call to worship, joyfully adored God, and then asked for forgiveness of our shortcomings in the light of God's goodness. Throughout this process, we are invested in God's worship and our faith spiritually, physically, and emotionally. We are now ready and seeking to hear from God. We wait for God's Word.

The reading of the Bible is the "main event" in worship. Why? Because as Christians, we are people of the Book. The Bible is at the center of Christian life. It's the big letter from God that tells us who we are, who God is, what Jesus has done for us, and what God is calling us to do. The Bible is our foundation from which everything is built, and we are admonished to read it aloud and in public. Paul tells Timothy to "give attention to the public reading of scripture" (1 Timothy 4:13).

Often a worship service will include more than one reading, with one of those readings being the central focus of the proclamation. The other readings, however, are just as important as the Scripture used in the sermon. The power of Scripture is not dependent on the interpretation of it through a sermon. It has value even if it stands alone as simply a reading of God's word.

Often, the reading of the Word is preceded by a prayer for illumination. This prayer asks God to open our minds and hearts and make us attentive to God's message to us. Once again, we acknowledge our dependence on God to learn and increase our faith.

The reading of Scripture is often just that: a reading. However, the reading of Scripture can also take on the form of liturgical movement, reader's theater, a drama, or a scripted reading. It is important, however, to keep in mind that if the goal is the reading of the Word, one must stay close to the text itself as read in the Bible. An interpretation of Scripture is for the proclamation. The reading of the Word presents the Biblical text as it stands in Scripture.

45

ACTIVITIES

1. Sculptures
(30–45 minutes, liturgical movement)

Adapted from "Sculpture Garden" and "Scripture Sculptures" in T.E.A.M.'s *All That We Are: An Arts and Worship Workbook.*

Supplies: A copy of the Scripture with the "movement words" highlighted

Preparation: Select a Scripture passage and then choose words in the passage that inspire movement. The best words are usually action words, words that evoke a feeling, or nouns. This activity usually works best with epistle passages or psalms (not as well with narratives). An example of Scripture prepared for this activity is:

> Make a **joyful** noise to the LORD, all the earth.
> **Worship** the LORD with gladness;
> Come into his presence with **singing.**
>
> **Know** that the LORD is **God.**
> It is he that made us, and we are his;
> We are his **people,** and the **sheep** of his pasture.
>
> Enter his gates with **thanksgiving,** and his courts with praise.
> Give thanks to him, **bless** his name.
>
> For the LORD is good; his steadfast **love** endures forever,
> And his **faithfulness** to all generations.
>
> Psalm 100

Directions: Tell the participants they are going to learn a new way of listening to the Scripture that involves more than just their ears. This way of listening involves all their senses. Begin with a couple of warm-up activities.

First, tell the group members that you are going to ask them to touch a certain color and they are to find that color on someone else. When you call out a new color, they do not have to keep touching the old color. Next tell them that you are going to name two body parts and they have to touch those two together with someone else in the group (like elbow to knee or head to head).

Now ask the group to divide into smaller groups of four. Tell the groups that they will be forming a sculpture garden and that each small group will be one of the sculptures in the garden. Tell the group that you are going to call out a word and count to five out loud. In those five beats, the group should move into a sculpture. Three rules must be observed:

1. No one can talk or instruct the group.
2. Each individual must be touching at least one other individual.
3. There is no right or wrong sculpture. Just do what comes naturally.

Begin with the following list of concrete words: lighthouse, tree, wave, church, car, volcano. After you say each word and the group has formed the sculpture, ask the participants to return to their circle facing one another to form another sculpture. They should always start from the circle. You may have to keep reminding the groups of the rules.

Next, use the following more abstract words: joy, fear, anger, love, baptism, Communion, worship. At this point, you may need to remind the groups that they are supposed to be one unified sculpture of the Word and not four little sculptures of the Word.

Now ask the groups to join together into one large group. Repeat the following words: lighthouse, church, joy, fear. (If you have a large group, then just ask the groups of four to join with another group to form a group of eight people. Scripture sculpture groups should not consist of more than eight or so people.)

Next, tell the group that you are going to call out a series of words that come from the Scripture reading for today. The rules are still the same for the sculpture, but, instead of breaking between sculptures, participants will move from one sculpture to the next. Go through the words a couple of times. Remind the participants that they do not have to do the same thing each time and, in fact, the sculptures will probably change naturally as they really begin to hear the words and think about what the words mean to them.

On the third time through, tell the youth you will read the Scripture and they should move into the sculpture when they hear the highlighted word. Tell them you will emphasize the highlighted word as you read the Scripture and pause for them to move into the sculpture. Go through the Scripture and liturgical movement (which is what they have created) twice—three times if you prefer.

If you have more than one Scripture sculpture group, ask the groups to show one another their sculptures. Watching another group can be just as instrumental in "hearing" the story as actually doing the movements.

To experience the Scripture in another movement scenario, read the Scripture first, and then have the group do the movement in silence or with instrumental music playing in the background. Do this only when and if the group members have become very familiar with their sculptures.

Discussion Questions: Now ask the group to sit in a circle and discuss the following questions:

1. How did you "hear" differently when you listened with your whole body instead of just your ears?
2. What are the messages you heard in the Scripture?
3. What is important about the Scripture?
4. Did you hear anything new?

At the end of the discussion, invite the participants to close their eyes and listen to the Scripture one more time. Read it very slowly as if it were a prayer. At the end, say "Amen."

2. Scripture on the Road
(1–3 hours, discussion)

Supplies: A Scripture reading, a mode of transportation, Bibles for each participant, journals or paper, pens/pencils, a copy of the discussion questions for each participant

Directions: Read the chosen Scripture passage in several different contexts. Read the Scripture in the van on the road, the mall, a quiet place outside, in the church sanctuary, in a homeless shelter, in front of a beautiful view of nature, in the church basement/attic, or a restaurant. Choose locations that are very different from each other (quiet, loud, no other people, lots of people, dark, light, wealthy area, poor area, etc.). Before leaving, distribute the journals/paper and pens/pencils and ask for volunteers to read the passage aloud in the different locations.

After each reading, ask the participants to take a moment and write some answers to the discussion questions you have given them. Remind them that they do not have to answer every question every time. The questions are meant to be a guide to their writing.

When you return, discuss what people wrote in their journals. Use the discussion questions to guide this session.

Discussion Questions:

1. Is it hard or easy to hear? Why?
2. Is it embarrassing or easy to read the Scripture here? Why?
3. Did I actually listen to the Scripture? If not, what distracted me?
4. What new thing did I hear in the Scripture in this place that I didn't hear before?
5. If this Scripture was actually being read to all the people in this place, what would they think? What would they hear?
6. Did I like listening to the Scripture here? Where do I prefer to hear the Scripture read?

3. Do What They Do
(time, place, and style dependent on chosen passage)

Supplies: Dependent on chosen Scripture reading

Directions: Choose a Scripture passage. Read the Scripture while doing the action described in the passage. In other words, bring the context of the story as alive as possible. If you are reading about the Israelites in the desert, read the Scripture while you are walking or hiking. Read about the Last Supper while eating a meal. Read the Creation Story while on a walk through the zoo or on a nature walk. While on a boat, read about the calling of Peter, James, and John or the story of Jesus walking on the water. Read about Israelite slavery while doing some heavy labor project. Read Paul's writings while in a jail cell.

After the reading, ask the youth how reading the Scripture passage in this context changed how they listened and what they listened for. What did they hear that was new in the Scripture?

4. Word Chant

(15 minutes, art)

Supplies: Paper, pens/pencils, newsprint, tape, a marker, any Scripture reading

Directions: Give each person a sheet of paper and a pen or pencil. Read the Scripture passage to the participants one time. Ask them to listen as you read the Scripture passage a second time and to write down any words that just seem to pop out at them.

Invite all the participants to share the words they wrote down by going around the circle. Ask a scribe to write the words on a sheet of newsprint posted on the wall. The scribe should make tick marks after any repeated words.

After everyone has shared, ask the participants to read aloud the words listed. The list of words will become the chant. For every tick mark beside a word, the group should repeat that word.

You may also bring percussion instruments (hand drums, triangles, maracas, jingle bells, cymbals, etc.). After the group has read through the words a few times and gotten the feeling of the chant, put a funky beat behind it and chant again or as much as you want. The group might even be inspired to get up and dance!

Discussion Questions:

1. What words were the most popular? Why?
2. Have the words chosen taken on a new importance?
3. What part of the Scripture passage does the chant seem to highlight?
4. Does the chant enhance, change, or distract from the Scripture passage? Why?

5. Playing with Role Play

(15–30 minutes, game/drama)

Supplies: Any Scripture reading

Directions: After the participants have read the Scripture passage together, invite them to revisit the Scripture in several different role-play styles. You may choose a few from the list that follows or do all the different role plays in the order listed. For each role play, encourage new volunteers to take over. Give each new group no more than five minutes to plan out what they will do. The role plays should be basically unrehearsed and spontaneous; the youth should not feel pressured to do a perfect reenactment of the Scripture.

If you have a very large group, divide the group into smaller groups and give each group one of the role-play options. Then, have the groups share them with one another.

Between role plays, ask the following questions:

1. Was the reenactment accurate?
2. What did the participants add or leave out?
3. If you saw something new in the story, what was it?

4. How does the story change when you act it out in a different way?

5. Are there parts of the story that seem more important or less important when acted out in this way?

Act out the story silently

Act out the story using dialogue

Act out the story in slow motion

Act out the story in fast motion

Act out the story backwards

Act out the story with a narrator as the only speaker

Act out the story in freeze frame action (form different sculptures to tell the story)

If you are using this activity outside of the worship setting, here are a few other role-play options. Act out the story opera style. Act out the story Shakespeare style. Act out the story using other genres, cultures, and time periods (for example, using teenage slang, acting it out in the Elizabethan time period, turning it into a poem where one actor must rhyme the preceding actor's sentence). These options are meant for Scripture readings with which it is appropriate to use humor; they are not meant to degrade or negate the text. Use your best judgment here. These options are meant to be simple, silly ways to help the participants learn and remember the passage.

6. Storyboard
(30 minutes, art)

Supplies: Copies of the chosen Scripture passage, art supplies

Preparation: Divide the Scripture passage where it naturally seems to transition in terms of the action or the description. For instance, the Creation Story could be divided by days. A psalm can often easily be divided by verse, by the change in mood, or by what the psalmist is describing. A story from the Gospels or Paul can be divided often by verse, but definitely by scenes or change in action. Be prepared to give each smaller group or individual in your group one of the segments of the passage.

Directions: Divide the group into pairs, threes, or individuals (depending on the size of your whole group). Give each smaller group a copy of the entire Scripture passage. Next, assign a segment of the passage to each group. Announce that each group is responsible for one frame in the storyboard of the Scripture. Explain that a storyboard is a visual telling of a story. Invite the participants to first read the entire Scripture passage and then draw, paint, glue, color, sculpt, and/or use whatever art supplies you have collected to make their part of the storyboard. After everyone has finished, put the different frames of the storyboard together in order. Ask the groups to explain their part of the storyboard in the sequence they appear.

This project can be as simple or as complex as you want it to be. Some groups may do this activity on one long piece of butcher paper with crayons. Other groups may paint separate banners representing each part of the Scripture. The important thing is to learn and remember the Scripture passage in a new way by becoming intimately involved in the telling of it.

7. Many Voices
(5–10 minutes, drama)

Supplies: Copies of the Scripture reading written in script form

Preparation: Write the Scripture in script form with the narrator and character parts identified.

Directions: Pass out the copies of the Scripture passage and ask for volunteers to play the different parts or characters identified in the passage. Often the hearing of the text can be significantly enhanced if the voices change as the story is told. For example, a female voice reading Mary's part contrasted with Joseph's male voice brings the text alive.

8. Responsive Reading
(5–10 minutes, drama)

Supplies: Copies of the Scripture reading written in script form with the different parts identified

Preparation: Divide the Scripture passage into different parts. The parts do not have to be based on the character's lines as in the "Many Voices" activity. Divide the parts by men, women, youth, adults, left, right, one, all, etc. You may also designate how the groups are to read them (whispering, shouting, happily, sadly, etc.).

Directions: Pass out the copies of the Scripture passage. Make note of the different parts that are identified in the passage. Read the text together following the instructions of who reads what. Often just changing the sound of the words by using various voices can bring the text alive in a new way or help people hear things they might not have heard before.

9. Gathering the Scripture
(30 minutes, game)

Supplies: Copies of the Scripture reading, copies of the list of elements that are identified in the Scripture passage

Preparation: This exercise is best used with a passage that names several objects that your group can actually find or collect on site. In other words, you wouldn't want to choose a psalm full of nature objects if you are meeting in an inner-city church at night.

Make a list of objects that are identified in the Scripture passage. If you are using a birth narrative, your list can include such items as hay, blankets, a lantern, and a feeding trough. If you are using Psalm 150, your list can include a trumpet, guitar, and cymbals. The Scripture might also inspire you to think of some modern-day objects that symbolize elements of the passage.

Directions: Give the participants a copy of the list of objects and ask them to collect as many things as they can find in fifteen minutes (longer if needed and time allows). Ask the group to put all the supplies in one central location. After everything has been collected, ask the participants to sit around the supplies. Discuss the following:

1. All of the supplies have something to do with one specific Scripture passage. Any guesses as to which one?
2. If you could choose a passage that had to do with all of these supplies, which would you choose?

Next, read the chosen Scripture passage. After reading it, ask the youth if they would change anything about what they gathered. Discuss how the presence of the objects changes or enhances what they hear when the Scripture passage is read.

10. *Lectio Divina*
(5–15 minutes, meditation)

Supplies: A Scripture passage

Directions: *Lectio divina* is a four-part process that consists of listening to the Scripture, meditating on the Scripture, praying to God in response to the Scripture, and listening to God's response. You may choose to use parts of the lectio divina or choose to do the whole process.

Reading is the first part. Invite the participants to find a comfortable place to sit, ask them to close their eyes, and instruct them to take a few slow, deep breaths. Tell them to clear their minds and concentrate only on the words of the Scripture. Ask them to listen to the Scripture not only with their head but with their heart. Then, read the passage slowly.

The second part, meditation, begins by slowly reading the Scripture again. Instruct the participants to listen for a certain word or phrase that seems to stand out or catch their attention. Ask them to repeat the one word or phrase over and over silently. Tell them to ponder the word, to think about it, and to pray for understanding. Wait a few minutes after you have finished reading the passage so that participants may meditate.

Speaking is the third part. Invite participants to respond to the Scripture through prayer. Ask them to pray whatever comes to mind after having listened to the Scripture and meditated upon it.

Finally, the last part is contemplation. Ask participants to silently contemplate God, listen for God, and think about God. Ask them to silently repeat God's name over and over, to let go of any expectations, and to simply experience God's presence. Ask them to listen for God's still, small voice in the silence.

Lectio divina may also be done by the participants themselves without a central leader. By letting participants lead the group, you enable the youth to proceed at their own pace. Either provide the instructions written here or let the participants guide themselves after they have experienced lectio divina a few times with a leader.

After you have completed the process, you may invite the participants to write in their journals or discuss what they experienced and share their thoughts. Another option is to simply continue in worship.

For more information, read about lectio divina in *Soul Feast,* by Marjorie J. Thompson, or Montreat Youth Conference's *Small Group Leader's Manual: Freed to Be,* by Karen Akin.

WORKS CITED

Akin, Karen. 1998. *Small Group Leader's Manual: Freed to Be.* Montreat, N.C.: Montreat Conference Center.

Thompson, Marjorie J. 1995. *Soul Feast: An Invitation to the Christian Spiritual Life.* Louisville, Ky.: Westminster John Knox Press.

CHAPTER 6

Proclamation of the Word

Now that we have read God's Word together, we seek to understand it. What does it have to do with our lives? What does it matter to us? How can it and will it change us? As hearers of the Word we wish to learn something new about a Scripture passage. We want to be informed about what the Bible is teaching us. We want to understand the message of Scripture and how it applies to our everyday life. We seek to hear the Word proclaimed and interpreted for the modern world in which we live.

In addition, hearers of the Word seek inspiration from the proclamation of Scripture. We want not only to be taught but also to be touched by the Word. Through proclamation, God not only fills our minds but also shapes our hearts. To focus on one aspect without the other is to leave the task of proclamation incomplete.

When we think of the proclamation time, we often imagine a sermon given by a pastor who stands in a pulpit and talks for fifteen or so minutes. However, throughout centuries of Christianity, God's Word has been proclaimed in many different ways, including visual art, drama, dance, stories, music, and the like. The proclamation can take on many different forms today, as well. Creativity in a proclamation is limited only by how it faithfully serves to communicate the Scripture and God's message to the congregation. The goal of a proclamation is to teach the Scripture so that others might learn and be inspired by God's Word.

Before a teacher can teach a subject, she must have studied it well. Before an inspirational speaker can touch someone else's heart, his heart must first be touched. Before a public speaker can give an effective speech, she must practice it. Three tasks, then, confront us when we prepare to proclaim God's word. One: We must study God's Word and seek to understand it. Two: We must pray God's Word and seek the Holy Spirit's inspiration. Three: We must craft how we will share our experience of study and prayer with others and practice it so we are prepared.

With our T.E.A.M. worship groups, we often talk about the first two tasks, study and prayer, in terms of "process versus product." It is often tempting to focus all the energy on the final *product* of the proclamation—what it will look like, what will be effective, what will be said, and who will do what parts. However, the most important piece of the proclamation is the *process* we take to get to that final product. This process is called "exegesis," literally meaning "to draw out." The steps taken to thoroughly study the Word, seek to understand it, and discover its modern application make up the process of exegesis—drawing out of the passage God's message to us.

If we focus too soon on the final product, we may be guilty of "eisegesis." Eisegesis literally means "to put in." It is tempting when reading a text—especially an exciting text—to immediately say, "I know exactly what this means!" Then, we fill the text with our own thoughts, plans, ideas, political or social agendas, and priorities. Eisegesis is reading into the passage what we want to see. Our job is to draw out and share what the text already says on its own, not what we want it to say.

A good example is a Reebok commercial that aired on TV a few years ago. The commercial featured pictures of several men and women with athletic, healthy, and beautiful bodies. The words "Your Body Is a Temple" appeared over the pictures. When we do a study of Paul's words, we understand that when Paul says "your body," he is speaking in the plural. "You" is not an individual "you" but a plural "you all." Thus, we can see how this text has been improperly interpreted by Reebok and by many others over time. Paul was speaking about the community and the character of the community, not about individual physical bodies.

Reebok used the Scripture for its own purposes (to sell a product). In proclamation, our job is to seek out God's purposes in order to proclaim God's Word. This is not to say that our opinions are not important. Our opinions can guide questions, energize us, and give us real modern-day issues to apply to the Scripture. However, our opinions should never be a replacement for what God has to say to us through the Scripture.

After exegesis (study and prayer) has been accomplished, the final product is ready to be formed. Now we can get excited about how we might communicate what we have learned. A good process sets your group securely on the right path for a faithful and effective proclamation of God's Word to the congregation before you.

ACTIVITIES

1. Exegesis Exercise
(1–2 hours, study/discussion)

Supplies: A Scripture passage, several different versions of the Bible (NRSV, NIV, CEV, Jerusalem Bible, NKJV, etc.), several different Bible Commentaries (*NIB, Interpretation, Barclay,* etc.), an Interlinear version of the Bible (which gives a direct translation of the verses from their original language), and Gospel parallels (if you are using a Gospel text, this tool tells you where to find the same story in the other Gospels), paper, pens/pencils, newsprint or chalkboard, markers, tape, copies of the Study Guide on pages 57–59.

Preparation: First, you and your group will need to choose a text to study. Then, gather the above supplies. Your pastor should be able to help you locate these items in your church library or the pastor's library. You may also ask your pastor, youth director, or Christian educator to be present during this activity. However, if you do so, make sure the person understands that he or she is not there to give all the answers but to guide the participants in the use of the reference material and to ask helpful questions in order to get the participants thinking.

Directions: Many tools are available to help draw out the message of a biblical text. In doing exegesis, keep in mind issues of the original language in which it was written (Greek or Hebrew), the culture or the overall context of the original audience of the text, the literary style and technique of the text, and where the text appears in the Bible. The following activity is designed to help youth discover these tools of exegesis and how to use them in studying Scripture.

After choosing a text, ask members of the group to take turns reading the text aloud, each using a different translation. Tell your group that as the text is being read each time, write down questions that you have about the text. The questions can be anything from "What is he talking about?" to "What is a tabernacle anyway?" to "What does this have to do with me?" After the text has been read in the different translations, ask people to share their questions. Write the questions on the newsprint or the chalkboard. Tell the youth to keep these questions in mind as they go through the rest of the activity.

Now, divide the group into five smaller groups. Assign one of the following topics to each group: historical/cultural context, biblical context, language issues, literary style, or allusions and parallels. With the supplies you have available, each group's job is to search for information regarding its assigned topic. The following is a guide for each group's study.

Gather the groups together. Ask each group to give a short report highlighting its findings. What did each group find that was interesting or significant? List their findings on the newsprint. Allow time between each group for others to ask questions or make comments.

After all the groups have reported, ask everyone to keep all the findings in mind. Then, ask each participant to write one sentence that would describe the overall "message of the text." Give them three to five minutes to do this silently. Then ask the participants to share their sentence and list them on another piece of newsprint.

Discuss the following questions:

1. What patterns or common themes appear in the sentences?

2. What differences are there?

End the activity by asking the group to read aloud together all of the sentences listed on the newsprint. Ask everyone to shout "Amen!" when the group has finished reading them.

Study Guide

Historical/Cultural Context

Some Bibles have an introduction for each book of the Bible. It can give helpful tips on the original audience, the characteristics of the author, and other information. Commentaries can also have helpful insights with these issues.

Use the following questions to guide your study:

1. What is the cultural situation in which the text was written or in which the events described took place?
2. Who was in power?
3. Where on the map did it take place?
4. What were the roles of the people involved?
5. Who was at odds with whom?
6. Who was the audience for this text?
7. What difference would it make?
8. From your answers, what message is the Scripture passage communicating?

Biblical Context

Read up to a chapter before and after your chosen text to get the full picture. Bible commentaries sometimes have insights into the perspective of your book and can give you clues when it comes to context.

Use the following questions to guide your study:

1. Where is this text situated in the Bible? Is it near the beginning of a book, toward the middle, or near the end of it?
2. What comes before your text? What comes after it?
3. How does the material around it affect the way you read it? (Example: If your text is a healing miracle of Jesus surrounded by other healings, the author may be trying to show the various kinds of people Jesus healed.)
4. From your answers, what message is the Scripture communicating?

Language Issues

You will need different translations of the Bible. The different translations can give clues to words that have questionable or variable translations. Some Bibles (such as the NRSV and the Oxford Annotated Study Bible) have footnotes that give alternate meanings or point out a lack of clarity in the translation. Some Bible commentaries also will include notes about certain words. If your pastor is a particularly good language scholar, ask him or her to review the text and tell you about any word issues he or she has found.

Use the following questions to guide your study:

1. Within the different translations, have particular words been translated differently?
2. Do you notice repeated phrases or patterns in the sentences?
3. Are there words that your group doesn't understand? Do some words have more than one meaning? (For instance, the Hebrew word for "spirit" also means "breath" and "wind.")
4. What words seem to jump out as "key words" in your text?
5. From your answers, what message is the Scripture communicating?

Literary Style

Sometimes the format of the text can give away a literary style. Prophecies, psalms, and other poetic styles are often written in an indented format. More poetic forms will be symbolic in nature, while narratives and historical writings are meant to be read more literally. Bible commentaries often comment on whether a given text is similar to or very different from other texts of the same literary style.

Use the following questions to guide your study:

1. What kind of writing is this text? Is it a narrative (an account of an event), a letter, a story, poetry, a dream, a vision, or something else?
2. What symbolism is being used?
3. What is the central metaphor?
4. How does the text fit the mold of a particular literary type? How does it break the mold?
5. What is the climax of the text?
6. What characters or what things are important in the text?
7. How does the kind of literature that is used affect the way we read and understand it? (Example: If you are reading a letter, you must keep in mind that it is someone else's mail and you probably won't understand all of the inferences made. You also must then try to learn something about the recipients of the letter and their particular situation.)
8. From your answers, what message is the Scripture communicating?

Parallels and Allusions

Some Bibles (such as the NRSV and the Oxford Annotated Study Bible) will have citations of scriptural parallels to the passage you are studying. Bible *(Study* commentators will often comment on the differences in how the same story is told in two different Gospels.

Many sayings of Jesus are quotes or allusions of Old Testament Scripture. Find any allusions that your text makes to other stories or sayings in the Bible.

Use the following questions to guide your study:

1. Does your text directly correlate or connect with another one in the Bible?
2. Why does the writer choose to include a certain allusion?
3. If it is an account that is found in the other Gospels, how is it the same or different?
4. What is the writer trying to emphasize compared to the other parallels?
5. What is the writer hoping to accomplish by using a certain allusion or quote?
6. From your answers, what message is the Scripture communicating?

2. Modern Parallels
(30–45 minutes, discussion/drama)

Supplies: A Scripture passage, Bibles, newsprint, markers, paper, pens/pencils

Directions: Ask the group to read the chosen text. Then, as a group, brainstorm modern situations that might parallel the text. For example, the good Samaritan story could be paralleled to a homeless person in your town who is passed over by an elder and a pastor. However, a person who would be looked down on in your community stops to help. Don't worry about the parallels being exactly perfect; they should just be similar enough to carry the same message. Write the ideas on the newsprint. After the youth have created a list of possible modern parallels, ask them to choose a few that they would like to explore.

Next, divide the group into smaller groups of four to six people and assign one of the modern parallels to each group. Ask the groups to create a short skit using the parallel. Give them about ten minutes to create their scenes.

Gather the groups back together and ask one volunteer to read the original Scripture passage from the Bible. Then, invite each group to share its scene. Between groups, allow time for the participants to ask questions, make comments, and show their appreciation.

3. Scripture Slogans
(30 minutes, discussion/art)

Supplies: A Scripture passage, Bibles, newsprint, markers, paper, pencils

Directions: Read the chosen passage aloud in the group. Discuss the following: What is God doing in this passage? What is the message to the people in this passage? What is God's message to us? This discussion can be enhanced if done after completing the exegesis activity. Write on newsprint the different ideas for the message of the text.

Now divide your group into smaller groups of three or four people. Ask them to brainstorm slogans for the message of the text. The slogan can be in the form of a bumper sticker, a T-shirt slogan, a jingle, a commercial, or something else. Groups can also use already familiar slogans used in music, commercials, and television series.

After about ten minutes, gather the groups back together and ask one volunteer to read the original Scripture passage from the Bible. Then, invite each group to share its slogan. Between groups, allow time for the participants to ask questions, make comments, and show their appreciation.

4. Dear Diary
(30 minutes, writing)

Supplies: A narrative Scripture passage, Bibles, paper, pens/pencils

Directions: Read the chosen passage aloud in the group. Next, ask each person to choose a character from the passage. It can be the main character mentioned, a minor character, a bystander in a crowd, or someone referred to but not present in the current story.

When everyone has chosen a character, tell your group that you are going to read the story again, but this time ask each person to pay special attention to how his or her character would perceive the action in the story. What is the character thinking or doing? What is the character feeling?

Next, ask the participants to write a diary entry from their character's perspective. It should include what they experienced and what they thought and felt about it.

After about fifteen minutes, gather the groups back together and ask one volunteer to read the original Scripture passage from the Bible. Then, invite participants to share their writings. Allow time for the participants to ask questions, make comments, and show their appreciation.

5. Bible Banners
(45–60 minutes, art)

Supplies: A Scripture passage, newsprint, markers, paper, pens/pencils, large piece of banner fabric (a sheet or piece of muslin), several scissors, glue (fabric or hot glue), paints (fabric or acrylic), paint supplies, scraps of fabric, felt, any other banner-making supplies, a rope and dowel rod to hang the banner

Directions: Select a Scripture passage and read the chosen passage aloud in the group. Discuss the following: What is God doing in this passage? What is the message to the people in this passage? What is God's message to us? This discussion can be enhanced if done after completing the first activity in this chapter (exegesis). Ask the group to brainstorm short sentences that capture the message of the text. Write them on the newsprint.

Next, give each person a piece of paper and a pencil and tell the youth to take five minutes to silently think of a visual way of describing the message of the text through a banner. Assure the participants that their drawings don't have to be perfect or ingenious, just enough to communicate an idea. Advise them to avoid using lots of words. Remind the youth that the best banners are usually simple in design.

Next, ask the group to come back together and invite people to show what they have designed and tell how it symbolizes the message of the text. After all who wish have shared, ask the group to look for common themes in the designs. Is there one design or a combination of designs that sum up the group's thoughts? Ask the group to create one design to use in a banner. Invite the youth to use the materials present to create a group banner that proclaims the text.

6. Critique the Preacher!
(30–40 minutes, discussion)

Supplies: One copy of the critique form for each participant, pens/pencils

Preparation: Ask for your pastor's cooperation in letting your group critique an upcoming sermon. Also, decide with your group if you should invite the pastor to your discussion of his or her sermon. The participants may be more comfortable with inviting the pastor after they have done this activity a few times and are familiar with the process.

This activity is most effective after doing the first activity in this chapter (exegesis) or some other in-depth Bible study.

Directions: Find out what text will be used in the sermon you are going to critique. If time allows, make arrangements to do an exegetical study of the text. Use the exegesis activity on pages 55–56. If time does not allow for this in-depth of a process, then ask a small group to gather and do the exegesis of the passage. Ask the small group to share its findings. Tell the participants that the pastor will be preaching and that the youth will have an opportunity to evaluate his or her performance.

Go over the critique form provided in this section and answer any questions the participants may have concerning the categories, words, or way the form is formatted. Remind them that preaching is an incredibly difficult task. This is not an opportunity to give your pastor a hard time, but rather a new way for the youth to experience a sermon and learn from it. Ask them to take notes during the sermon and fill out the form. Remind them that they will have to listen carefully.

After worship, assemble the group again and go over everyone's answers to the questions on the completed forms. It will be important for you to keep the discussion focused on the task at hand. Remind the youth that the point is not to talk about how boring the music was or how the pastor's outfit looked. Use the critique form to help the group stay focused.

Discuss the following questions:

1. What did you learn in the sermon?
2. What did you agree with? What did you disagree with?
3. What about the sermon was helpful or not helpful to you?
4. If you had preached this sermon, what would you have made sure to say?

After the discussion, end with a prayer thanking God for God's Word, for the pastor's sermon, and for the continued interpretation of the Word through your discussion.

7. Video Interview
(2–3 hours, art)

Supplies: A Scripture passage (choose a passage that tells a story for this activity), Bibles, newsprint, markers, paper, pens/pencils, a video camera for every six people, blank videotape, props, costumes, a television and cables to play the video

Directions: Read the chosen passage aloud in the group. Discuss the following: What is God doing in this passage? What is the message to the people in this passage? What is God's message to us? This discussion can be enhanced if it occurs after the exegesis activity (pp. 55–56).

Ask the group to name the characters in the passage and list them on the newsprint. Don't forget to include people who are in supporting roles (such as members of the crowd or unnamed disciples in the story). For each character, discuss the following:

1. What does the person want?
2. What are his or her motivations and reactions?

The Critique Form

What passage did the preacher use in his or her sermon?

What new things did you learn about the passage from the sermon? (Use the following categories, but don't expect something new in every category. Sermons often will focus on a few key things in certain areas.)

    Historical/cultural context: (the life situation of the people in the text)

    Biblical context: (where the passage is located in the Bible)

    Language issues: (key words or phrases used in the passage)

    Literary style: (What kind of writing is this? Poetry? A story?)

    Allusions and parallels: (Does this passage connect to or parallel other passages?)

The preacher really had my attention when . . .

The preacher really lost my attention when . . .

What I will remember most about this sermon is . . .

Use three words to describe the sermon.

From what you heard in the sermon, what does this passage have to do with you and your life?

3. What was the person thinking as the action of the story unfolded?

4. How did the character change as the story unfolded?

5. How was the character's faith born, enhanced, or diminished in the story?

6. Do you identify with this character? Why?

After discussing the characters, ask each group member to choose a character. Make sure each participant has a different character. Invite the group members to write a monologue (only a couple of paragraphs long) from their character's perspective that recounts their experience of what happened in the passage. Assign one group member the role of the interviewer and have that person write a short introduction as a news reporter covering the story of this passage.

As group members finish their monologue, ask them to meet with the interviewer to adjust their monologue into a question-and-answer format. When everyone has prepared his or her script, have the groups practice reading the scripts, choosing costumes and props to go with their scripts, and recording them on videotape. You can be as simplistic or as elaborate as you want. If you have a large group, you may want to break it into two casts creating two videos. Remember, you'll need two video cameras for that!

View your final product and then discuss what group members learned about the text and its characters.

8. Video Documentary
(2 sessions: 2–3 hours each, art)

Supplies: A Scripture passage (choose a passage that tells a story for this activity), Bibles, newsprint, markers, paper, pencils, copies of the chosen parts from Bible commentaries, a video camera, a blank videotape, a television and cables to play the video

Preparation: Find some Bible commentaries in your church or local library. Your pastor probably has a collection as well. Skim the commentaries looking for helpful insights to the chosen passage. Make copies of the helpful insights for the participants to read during the group discussion.

Directions: Read the chosen passage aloud in the group. Then discuss the following questions with the participants and print their answers on newsprint. This discussion can be enhanced if it occurs after completing the exegesis activity (pp. 55–56).

Discussion Questions:
1. Who are the characters in the passage?

2. What happens in the passage?

3. What are the cultural norms and customs of the situation? How do they affect what is happening in the passage?

4. Ask for volunteers to read aloud helpful information from the commentaries. Ask participants to put the commentator's words into their own words.

5. What is the overall message of the passage?

6. What significance does this passage have in our lives?

After the discussion, outline as a group how the passage might look if it were shown as a video documentary (like on PBS, the Discovery Channel, or The Learning Channel). Start by discussing the typical formulas and flows of a documentary. For example, the narrator has a clever introduction that introduces the place and time period, then he or she introduces a particular situation typical of the period. Finally, action shifts to period characters in dialogue. Another example is the documentary that recounts a story through flashback scenes. In between the scenes are commentaries by various professionals (such as scientists, historians, or other experts).

Ask the participants to choose a flow and complete the outline for their documentary of the passage they are studying. When the outline of the documentary has been completed, assign two people to each part of the outline and ask them to write a script for it. If you are working with a very large group, you may want to have more than one "cast" to produce two or more videos on the same Scripture.

When the scripts are written, read through them as a group. Make adjustments as needed to provide a smooth flow. You may choose one person with talent or interest in video to decide how the scenes will be filmed (including angles, pans, zooms, and effects). Then choose costumes and props. Practice running the scenes and how they will be filmed. Finally, record and have fun! View your final product and then discuss what group members learned about the text and its characters.

The decision on how much work you will do at each session depends on you and your group. Find an appropriate time to break before filming the second session.

For an extra "professional" look, locate someone in your church who has a computer or access to a computer that has video-editing capabilities. Many computer programs are now available that provide professional-quality editing.

9. Video Montage
(3 sessions: 1 hour each, art)

Supplies: A Scripture passage, Bibles, newsprint, markers, video cameras, video tapes, television, two VCRs (or video editing machine/computer), blank videotapes
Directions:
Session One: Read the chosen passage aloud in the group. Discuss the following: What is God doing in this passage? What is the message to the people in this passage? What is God's message to us? This discussion can be enhanced if done after completing the exegesis activity (pp. 55–56).

After studying the text and discussing its content and meaning, ask the group members to close their eyes as you read the passage to them again. Invite them to "run the visual" as you "run the audio." In other words, ask them to provide the pictures to the words that you read. What images come to mind? What do they see as you read? For example, the image that comes to mind might be a scene in nature or a modern parallel of the text. It could be something very concrete or very abstract. If a music video provides a picture to a song, then they are providing the picture to the Scripture.

After reading the text, ask the group members to share their images as you write them on the newsprint. As they share, take time to discuss how their images relate to the text.

Next, tell the youth that together, they will be making a video montage (collection of short clips) that reflects the passage. The ideas and images listed on the newsprint will serve as the outline or storyboard for the montage. Read the text again, stopping verse by verse to choose particular images on the newsprint that correspond to the particular verses. Also note which images give an overall picture rather than a specific image of the text. They could be used at the beginning or end of the montage.

After completing your video storyboard of images (your outline of the video montage), review the images list and do a quick "reality check." Which images can you realistically record on a camcorder or find in some footage? (For example, someone in the group might have a vacation home movie of a beach sunset that you wouldn't be able to readily film in your area.) Finally, make any last adjustments to the outline and decide how the passage will be read—before, after, or during the montage. Assign who will be responsible for what video clips.

Session Two: Ask group members to bring their video clips and show them to the group in the order that they would be seen in the montage. After viewing the clips, ask if the group wants to make any adjustments to the footage or the order. After the group feels comfortable with the montage, give the project to one or two group members who will put it together on one videotape. This can be done by connecting two VCRS (or a VCR and a video camera). It can also be done by using a video-editing machine or computer. Many home computers have this capability. Another option is to find someone in your church who works at the local television station or has access to a college film or journalism department with editing equipment.

Session Three: After the editing has been done, gather the group for the "Video Montage" premier! Ask for the group's reflections on the montage, the passage, and the process of making the video by discussing the following questions:

1. What did you learn about this passage by doing this activity?
2. How does this montage change or reinforce your perspective on the passage?
3. What did you learn about yourself and others by putting this video together?

10. Compilation Medley
(3 sessions: 30–45 minutes each, art)

Supplies: A Scripture passage, Bibles, tape player/CD player, various CDs/tapes, blank tape/rewriteable CD, newsprint, markers

Directions:
Session One: Read the chosen passage aloud in the group. Discuss the following: What is God doing in this passage? What is the message to the people in this passage? What is God's message to us? This discussion can be enhanced if done after completing the exegesis activity (pp. 55–56).

After studying the text and discussing its content and meaning, ask the group members to close their eyes as you read the passage to them again. Tell them that as they listen to it, they are to think about songs they know that relate to the passage and its meaning. They can be Christian or secular songs.

Ask the group members to share their songs as you write them on the newsprint. As they share, take time to discuss how their songs relate to the text. Then ask the group members to look at their music collections for songs that reflect the message of the text. Invite them to bring their music to the next meeting.

Session Two: Read the chosen passage again to refresh participants' memories. Invite the youth to share the songs they found. Play all or parts of the songs, or simply read particular lyrics. Write a list of the songs on the newsprint. After everyone has shared, ask the participants to outline a music medley by using portions of the songs they have heard. Ask one person in the group to be in charge of the actual recording. He or she can record onto a tape easily with most portable players as long as you have a CD player with two tape players. Otherwise, the recorder will need to take notes on where each song clip begins and ends, and then make arrangements to record later.

Session Three: After the editing has been done, gather the group members to listen to their music compilation medley. Ask for the group's reflection on the medley, the passage, and the process of making the medley by discussing the following questions:

1. What did you learn about this passage by doing this activity?
2. How does this medley change or reinforce your perspective on the passage?
3. What did you learn about yourself and others by putting this medley together?

11. Sermon Collage
(1 hour, art)

Supplies: A Scripture passage, Bibles, many magazines (several for each participant), glue, scissors, construction paper or poster board

Directions: Read the chosen passage aloud in the group. Discuss the following: What is God doing in this passage? What is the message to the people in this passage? What is God's message to us? This discussion can be enhanced if done after completing the exegesis activity (pp. 55–56).

Next, ask participants to browse through the magazines and cut out words and pictures that describe the meaning of the passage. Invite each person to create a collage on a piece of construction paper or poster board. Ask the youth to write the Scripture passage on their collage (around the edge, in the middle, or wherever they prefer).

After the participants have completed the collages, ask them to share their creations and explain how each collage depicts their understanding of the passage. After everyone shares, allow time for others to ask questions, make comments, and show their appreciation.

12. Proclamation Tunes

(30 minutes, writing)

Supplies: A Scripture passage, Bibles, pencils, paper, list of tunes

Preparation: Prepare a list of simple and familiar tunes (children's songs, church songs, choruses, or current pop hit songs). Some suggestions are "Mary Had a Little Lamb," "Jesus Loves Me," "Happy Birthday," "The Wheels on the Bus," "The Barney Song," the Doxology, "Row Your Boat," "The Itsy, Bitsy Spider," or the Gloria.

Directions: Read the chosen passage aloud in the group. Discuss the following: What is God doing in this passage? What is the message to the people in this passage? What is God's message to us? This discussion can be enhanced if done after completing the exegesis activity (pp. 55–56).

Next divide your group into groups of three to five people. Distribute the pens/pencils and paper. Assign each group a different, simple tune. Tell each group that it has fifteen minutes to come up with new lyrics that reflect the message of the passage. Assure the youth that they do not have to be brilliant. Tell them to just have fun with it and give it a shot. If time permits, ask the groups to make up motions for their songs as well.

After the groups have finished, ask them to take turns sharing their songs with the other groups. If you have some particularly shy folks or "non-singers," the whole group can sing each song instead of each small group "performing" for the others. Provide newsprint or overhead sheets for the groups to write their lyrics.

CHAPTER 7

Affirmation of Faith

When we say the affirmation of faith in worship, we are expressing our faith as a community, a church. Our words of belief are our first response to all that we have experienced in worship thus far. God has acted through calling us, forgiving us, and giving us the gift of God's Word read and proclaimed. Now it is our turn to respond to God's actions and gifts by saying what it is that we believe. After hearing God's Word and the proclamation, we are moved to stand and shout "Amen!" We do this by saying creeds and confessions of our church together.

The PC(USA)'s Directory for Worship (basically the rule book for Presbyterian worship) encourages us to use one of the official creeds of the Presbyterian Church found in the *Book of Confessions*. We are especially to use one of these approved creeds or confessions during services that include baptism or Communion (*Book of Order* W-3.3603). In corporate worship, we are unifying ourselves with the whole church—as in the church universal (past, present, and future). This means we use creeds that the whole church universal has agreed to use, believe in, and stand by.

This does not, however, mean that we can never say what we personally believe in our own words. Nor does it mean that we cannot design as a local church or youth group a statement of faith of our own. The Directory for Worship also states that a church confesses its faith in relation to "its particular heritage and its local situation" (*Book of Order* W-2.2009). The creeds and confessions simply serve as a tool that allows us all to buy into one set of historic, faith-filled words that we all believe to be important. Many churches use the Apostles' Creed, but many more creeds and confessions are found in the PC(USA)'s *Book of Confessions*.

So what are we to do when the words of these creeds and confessions often sound antiquated or irrelevant? Do we toss them aside and count them as a worthless routine we must recite every week like robots? Absolutely not! We use our brains and energy to understand what they say and how they are relevant to us. Many of the activities in this chapter are designed to help young people interpret the creeds and confessions into their own language so that they might understand them better.

The affirmation of faith is most often said in unison or responsively. This affirmation is symbolic of our strength as a community of faith. Our strength comes in our relationship with one another through Jesus Christ. When one person is struggling in his or her faith and may not even be able to say what he or she believes, another person whose faith is strong can say it for that person. Thus, the first person can rely on the second. We can count on the faith community in good times and in bad.

ACTIVITIES

1. Back to the Future
(15–30 minutes, writing)

Supplies: Copies of the creed phrases (one for each participant), creed phrase strips, hat or basket, newsprint

Preparation: Copy the creed phrases and cut each phrase into its own strip. Fold the strips and place them in a basket or hat. Also make copies of the creed phrases sheet as a whole for each participant to review.

Directions: Invite each participant to choose a strip of paper from the basket or hat. Ask the youth to open the paper and read what it says. Invite each person to think of a way of saying his or her creed phrase in modern language. In other words, if the paper says, "I believe in the Holy Ghost who spoke by the prophet," the person might say, "I believe in the Holy Spirit who uses the prophets to talk to people."

After a moment, go around the circle asking each person to read his or her creed phrase and modern phrase. If participants have trouble putting the statement in their own words, solicit help from the rest of the group. Write the modern phrases on a sheet of newsprint.

Distribute the creed phrase sheets. Discuss the following questions:

1. Which creed phrases are easy to understand?
2. Which creed phrases are confusing?
3. Which statements relate to your understanding of God?
4. Which statements are new, foreign, or conflicting to your understanding of God?
5. How are these creed phrases relevant to living out your faith on a daily basis?

2. We Believe Banner
(30–45 minutes, art)

Supplies: Copies of the creed phrase sheet, banner material (a sheet or a large piece of muslin or canvas), washable paint, paper plates or pie tins, paper towels or wipes, markers, newspaper or drop cloth, paint brushes

Preparation: Place banner material on a drop cloth or newspaper. Distribute paint onto plates (one color per plate). Make copies of the creed phrase sheet.

Creed Phrases

I believe in God the Father Almighty, Maker of heaven and earth.

(Apostle's Creed 2.1)

We confess and acknowledge one God alone, to whom alone we must cleave.

(The Scots Confession 3.01)

(God) is eternal, infinite, immeasurable, incomprehensible, omnipotent, invisible.

(The Scots Confession 3.01)

The cause of good works, we confess, is not our free will, but the Spirit of the Lord Jesus, who dwells in our hearts by true faith.

(The Scots Confession 3.13)

I belong—body and soul, in life and in death—not to myself but to my faithful Savior, Jesus Christ.

(The Heidelberg Catechism 4.001)

For by nature, I am prone to hate God and my neighbor.

(The Heidelberg Catechism 4.005)

The church is an assembly of the faithful called or gathered out of the world; a communion, I say, of all saints.

(The Second Helvetic Confession 5.125)

God hath life, glory, goodness, blessedness, in and of himself; and is alone in and unto himself all-sufficient.

(The Westminster Confession of Faith 6.012)

Sin is any want of conformity unto, or transgression of, the law of God.

(The Shorter Catechism 7.014)

Man's chief and highest end is to glorify God, and fully enjoy him forever.

(The Larger Catechism 7.111)

We reject the false doctrine, as though there were areas of our life in which we would not belong to Jesus Christ, but to other Lords.

(The Declaration of Barmen 8.15)

To be reconciled to God is to be sent into the world as his reconciling community.

(The Confession of 1967 9.31)

Like a mother who will not forsake her nursing child, like a father who runs to welcome the prodigal home, God is faithful still.

(The Brief Statement of Faith 10.3, lines 49–51)

I believe in the Holy Ghost; the holy catholic Church; the communion of saints; the forgiveness of sins; the resurrection of the body; and the life everlasting.

(Apostle's Creed 2.3)

As we believe and confess the Scriptures of God sufficient to instruct and make perfect the man of God, so do we affirm and avow their authority to be from God, and not to depend on men or angels.

(The Scots Confession 3.19)

[The Son of God (is) called Jesus, which means Savior] because he saves us from our sins, and because salvation is to be sought or found in no other.

(The Heidelberg Catechism 4.029)

[I am called a Christian] because through faith I share in Christ and thus in his anointing, so that I may confess his name, offer myself a living sacrifice of gratitude to him, and fight against sin and the devil with a free and good conscience throughout this life and hereafter rule with him in eternity over all creatures.

(The Heidelberg Catechism 4.032)

It is impossible for those who are ingrafted into Christ by true faith not to bring forth the fruit of gratitude.

(Heidelberg Catechism 4.064)

For we teach and believe that this Jesus Christ our Lord is the unique and eternal Savior of the human race, and thus of the whole world.

(The Second Helvetic Confession 5.077)

We call this Church catholic because it is universal, scattered through all parts of the world, and extended unto all times, and is not limited to any times or places.

(The Second Helvetic Confession 5.126)

By the decree of God, for the manifestation of his glory, some men and angels are predestined unto everlasting life, and others fore-ordained to everlasting death.

(Westminster Confession of Faith 6.016)

They whom God hath accepted in his Beloved, effectually called and sanctified by his Spirit, can neither totally nor finally fall away from the state of grace: but shall certainly persevere therein to the end, and be eternally saved.

(Westminster Confession of Faith 6.094)

The purest churches under heaven are subject both to mixture and error: and some have so degenerated as to become apparently no churches of Christ. Nevertheless, there shall be always a Church on earth, to worship God according to his will.

(Westminster Confession of Faith 6.144)

Justification is an act of God's free grace, wherein he pardoneth all our sins, and accepteth us as righteous in his sight, only for the righteousness of Christ imputed to us, and received by faith alone.

(The Shorter Catechism 7.033)

In life and death we belong to God.

(Brief Statement of Faith 10.1, line 1)

Through the grace of our Lord Jesus Christ, the love of God, and the communion of the Holy Spirit, we trust in the one triune God, the Holy One of Israel, whom alone we worship and serve.

(Brief Statement of Faith 10.1, lines 2–6)

The Spirit justifies us by grace through faith, sets us free to accept ourselves and to love God and neighbor, and binds us together with all believers in the one body of Christ, the Church.

(Brief Statement of Faith 10.4, lines 54–57)

The Constitution of the Presbyterian Church (U.S.A.), Part I, *Book of Confessions,* (Louisville, Ky: Office of the General Assembly, Presbyterian Church (U.S.A.), 1999).

Directions: This activity is an excellent follow-up to the Back to the Future activity presented above. Distribute the copies of the creed phrase sheet. Ask the group to discuss the phrases by defining them or figuring out what they mean. Then, ask the participants to discuss what the phrases mean to them personally and as a group.

Next, invite the group to make a "We Believe Banner." Ask each person to choose one of the creed phrases that he or she likes or is particularly drawn to. After the participants have chosen a phrase, invite them to add their handprint to the banner and then write their name and creed phrase next to their handprint. They can be as creative as they want. After everyone has contributed to the banner, ask the group to stand in a circle around the banner. Ask each participant to read the phrase they chose. At the end, have everyone shout "Amen!"

3. Good News Report

Supplies: The PC(USA)'s *Book of Confessions* (or copies of your denomination's creeds and confessions), Bibles, pens/pencils, paper

Preparation: Choose three or four creeds or confessions for the group to research.

Directions: Divide the group into smaller groups of two to four people. Assign each group a confession or creed. Ask the groups to read the introductory material provided before each confession or creed in the *Book of Confessions*. Provide Bibles for them to look at Scripture that their confession or creed may reference. Once they have done the research on the creed, ask the groups to write a synopsis of the introduction in a news report style. Encourage them to be creative. For example, a group might include "news footage" by acting out anything that has to do with its assigned confession or creed. The group might also do an interview.

Gather the groups together and invite them to share. Allow time between each group for the other participants to ask questions, make comments, and show their appreciation.

4. Statement of Faith Journal
(2 sessions: 45 minutes each, art/writing)

Supplies: Newsprint, markers, copies of the Apostles' or Nicene Creed (or another if you choose), copy paper (for homemade journals), notebooks (any size works for store-bought journals), construction paper, glue, tape, scissors, stapler, embroidery thread, big needles, hole punch, yarn, crayons, markers, magazines, paint, stickers, other art supplies for decorating the journals

Preparation: Choose seven phrases from the creed phrases on pages 71–73. Also, choose some corresponding Bible verses. Write them on newsprint and post the newsprint on the wall. Place the journal and art supplies on a table where they are easily accessible for the young people.

Directions:
Session One: Follow the directions for making journals in the Prayer Journal activity (pp. 30–31). Then, ask the participants to write down the creed phrases and Scripture references you have chosen. They should write one creed and/or Scripture reference on a page. Ask them to think and write about the creed phrases and Scripture references by spending a little time with their journal each

day over the next week. Tell them this is not a formal assignment—no pressure. They should use the journals to write down whatever comes to mind about what they believe, their faith, the questions they have, what the creeds and Scriptures mean to them, or anything else that strikes them based on the phrases and Scriptures you gave them. They can draw, write poetry, write a story, free write, make a collage, and so forth. Make sure that you tell them the only person who will read this journal will be themselves. They will be asked to share their experience with the journal at the next session, but how much they share will be up to each individual. If you are using this activity at a retreat or lock-in, set aside time for journal writing.

Session Two: Gather together after one week. Ask the participants to look through their journal and mark the highlights (the realizations, key questions, things they really like from their journal, etc.). Next, ask the participants to find a partner. Invite them to discuss what they thought of the experience and how it was helpful. Then, ask them to share some of the highlights they have marked. Remind the youth that they have permission to share only as much as they want (from reading a passage to just mentioning a theme they explored).

Gather the group together and invite each participant to use his or her journal entries to write a short statement of faith. Remind the participants that the statement of faith applies only to what they know today. Ask them to focus on what they believe about God, Jesus Christ, the Holy Spirit, and the church. Give them ten minutes to write their thoughts and beliefs, and then ask them to return to their partner, share their faith statements, and discuss how the faith statements are similar or different.

Now gather everyone back into the large group and read the Apostles' or Nicene Creed together. Discuss how the various statements compare to the creed. What are the similarities or differences?

To close, ask the group to stand in a circle. Open the prayer by inviting participants to share something out loud or silently from their journals or their statements of faith. Close the prayer in thanks to God for our growing and enduring faith.

5. Who and What
(30 minutes, discussion)

Supplies: Copies of a creed or confession of your denomination (one for each participant), pens/pencils, paper, newsprint, markers

Preparation: Make copies of a creed or confession that you wish to use. Write at the top of a sheet of newsprint or chalkboard the following questions: Who is Jesus? Who is God? Who is the Holy Spirit? What is the role of Scripture? What about baptism? What is the church? (Write one question per sheet.)

Directions: Distribute copies of the creed or confession to each participant. Read the creed aloud in the group. If you have chosen a particularly long one, you may want to divide it into sections and answer each question according to its corresponding statement. Ask the participants to find answers to the questions on the newsprint. Write their responses below the questions on the newsprint. Once all the questions have been answered, divide the group into smaller groups of three.

Invite the groups to write a statement of faith in their own words based on the responses to the questions on the newsprint.

Gather the groups together and ask them to share their faith statements. Discuss the following:

1. What sections of the creed meant the most to you? Why?
2. In what ways does the creed say what you believe?
3. Why might it be important for the church to make this statement?

6. First Word/Last Word
(20 minutes, writing)

Supplies: Paper, pens/pencils, markers, newsprint or chalkboard

Preparation: Write the following example on a sheet of newsprint or chalkboard and post it in the room where you will meet:

> I believe in God.
> God is great.
> Greatness comes from God.

Directions: Invite the youth to think for a couple of minutes about what they believe is true about God, Jesus, or the Holy Spirit. Ask them to share out loud some of the things they believe. Tell them this is a "no pressure" activity. They do not have to give a speech. Encourage participants to share just a phrase or a sentence. It may be helpful to recite the Apostles' Creed together in order to help them begin to think in this way.

Now invite them to write a three-sentence/phrase statement of faith. The structure is as follows. Refer to the example as you explain the directions.

1. The first sentence/phrase should state something they believe in.
2. The next sentence/phrase uses the last word of the first sentence/phrase as the beginning word of the second sentence/phrase. This sentence describes what they believe.
3. Again, the third sentence/phrase begins with the last word of the previous sentence/phrase. This sentence can further describe what they believe.

After the youth have finished, invite them to share their faith statements with the whole group or with a partner. If they do not wish to share their whole statement, they can always share the first and last words of their statements. After each person shares, allow time for others to ask questions, make comments, and show their appreciation.

7. Circle of Belief
(5 minutes, game)

Directions: Gather the participants in a circle and ask them to take a few moments to think about their faith journey. Ask them to think about what they believe about faith, church, God, Jesus, and the Holy Spirit. Then invite the participants to go around the circle with each person saying, "I believe . . ." See how many times the youth can go around the circle offering different belief statements. If someone needs help, invite the group to ask questions to get that person to think of a belief.

If your group needs a challenge, repeat the game, but put a time limit on them (three minutes). See how many times they can go around the circle, allowing them to repeat statements that were made the first time.

8. Creed Trivia
(15 minutes, game)

Supplies: Several copies of the *Book of Confessions* (one for each participant) or copies from a few creeds or confessions of your denomination

Preparation: Ask your pastor, youth minister, or Christian educator to help you collect copies of the *Book of Confessions.* You may find copies in your church library or presbytery resource center. You may also be able to borrow copies from session members.

Next, make a list of ten to twenty questions from the *Book of Confessions.* This game is designed to be like the old-time Bible drills, but instead of the Bible, it uses the *Book of Confessions.* Create questions according to a certain theme (God, the church, the role of Scripture) or one or two confessions. A sample question might be, "What is the role of Scripture?" This gives the participants the opportunity to explore one theme in depth by answering from any creed or confession. Another question might be, "In the Larger Westminster Catechism, what is the answer to the question, 'What is the Word of God?'" This gives the participants the opportunity to explore one creed or confession in depth.

Directions: Distribute the confessions to the members of your group. Explain that you are going to ask a question. The first person to find the answer should raise his or her hand and/or shout "Ding!" Ask for the answer and where the person found it. Give the other groups the opportunity to share any answers they found. Instead of awarding points, give the person who found the answer first a free pass on the next question. This will keep one person from dominating the game. Another option is to divide the group into smaller groups of two or three people to find the answers.

9. Brief Statement of Faith Visual Design
(45 minutes, art)

Supplies: Copies of A Brief Statement of Faith—Presbyterian Church (U.S.A.) found in the *Book of Confessions* (or a confession/creed from your denomination), construction paper, glue, scissors, paint, markers, modeling clay, yarn, tape, paint brushes, cups, paper towels, newspaper, other art materials

Preparation: Gather the art supplies. Divide and place them on several different tables so participants have plenty of space to work. Make copies of A Brief Statement of Faith.

Directions: Gather your group and read A Brief Statement of Faith aloud in the group. The statement is divided into three main paragraphs: one on Jesus, one on God, and one on the Holy Spirit. Ask participants to choose one of the paragraphs that appeals to them. Invite them to silently read their paragraph again and think about it for five minutes. You may want to play soft instrumental music in the background to encourage silent thought.

Then, invite the youth to move to the tables and create a visual reflection or response to their paragraph. Tell them they will have twenty minutes to create something with the art supplies provided. Remind the participants that the point is not to create a masterpiece but to simply create something that is a reflection or response to their paragraph. Artists and non-artists alike can participate in this activity.

Give time warnings throughout the twenty-minute period. After everyone has finished, ask the participants to share what they made in small groups or with the whole group. After each person shares, allow time for others to ask questions, make comments, and show their appreciation.

10. Collage of What You Believe
(30 minutes, art)

Supplies: A wide variety of magazines, glue, scissors, markers, colored pencils, construction paper, several copies of the PC(USA)'s *Book of Confessions* (one for each participant) or copies from a few creeds or confessions of your denomination

Preparation: Ask your pastor, youth minister, or Christian educator to help you collect copies of the *Book of Confessions.* You may find copies in your church library or presbytery resource center. You may also be able to borrow copies from session members.

Directions: Gather the group together and explain the purpose and rationale of the affirmation of faith using the introduction found at the beginning of this chapter. Next, distribute the construction paper (one piece for each participant) and the books. Ask participants to explore the *Book of Confessions* and choose four statements from it that they believe. Tell them to write one of the four statements on each of the four sides of the paper. Next, invite them to browse through the magazines and cut out pictures or symbols (or they can draw symbols) that represent the statements they chose.

After everyone has finished, invite the participants to share their collages by showing them and reading the statements they chose. Include a time for group members to share their designs with a partner or the whole group. After each person shares, allow time for others to ask questions, make comments, and show their appreciation.

11. Faith Extremes
(20–30 minutes, game)

Supplies: Masking tape, copies of A Brief Statement of Faith—Presbyterian Church (U.S.A.) found in the *Book of Confessions* (or a confession/creed from your denomination)

Preparation: Choose several phrases or sentences from A Brief Statement of Faith. Place an X (with masking tape) in the center of the room or space you are using.

Directions: Invite the group to make a huge circle with the X in the middle. Everyone should be standing far away from the X. Tell the group that you are going to read some faith statements. After each one, the participants should move to the very center of the circle on the X if they absolutely, 100 percent can confidently believe or live by the statement you read. If they absolutely, 100 percent do not think they can believe or live by the statement you read, they should stand where they are now—the very outside of the circle. Otherwise, they can choose any place between where they stand now and the X in the middle to show how they feel. In other words, they are going to place themselves on a continuum of what they believe.

Discussion Questions: After the game, pass out copies of A Brief Statement of Faith and discuss the following questions either in small groups or as one large group. To make the most of this session, encourage the participants to talk not in generalities but in specifics. Discourage talking solely in hypotheticals. Encourage discussion about their real-life experiences.

1. What statements did you feel the most confident about? Why?
2. Which ones do you have questions about?
3. What are your questions?
4. Did you find yourself most often on the X or toward the outside of the circle?
5. What do we need to find ourselves more and more on the X?

12. Radical Word of Belief
(20 minutes, discussion/art)

Supplies: Copies of statements from the Theological Declaration of Barmen found in the PC(USA)'s *Book of Confessions*

Preparation: Read the introduction to Barmen found in the *Book of Confessions*. Make notes in order to review the history to this confession with your group. Then, browse through Barmen looking for statements that would have been particularly strong or radical for that day. Make a list of the statements you chose and make copies for each participant.

Directions: Review the history of the Theological Declaration of Barmen and explain that many of the theologians and people who wrote our creeds and confessions often lived in radical times and wrote radical statements of belief. Distribute copies of the list of statements you made. Review each statement with the group. Ask the youth how they think the statement would have been radical at the time. Then, ask them if and how the statement is important for our time.

Divide the group into smaller groups of three. Assign one statement to each group. Ask the participants to design a symbol or logo that reflects their statement. After everyone has finished, gather the groups together and ask them to share their symbols or logos. After each group shares, allow time for others to ask questions, make comments, and show their appreciation.

CHAPTER 8

Prayers of the People
and the Lord's Prayer

The prayers of the people combine to form the longest prayer of worship. It can go by many names. Regardless of what you call it—prayers for the people, prayers of petition, or prayers of intercession and supplication—it usually has the same purpose. Just like all other parts of worship, the congregation takes an active role by praying along with the leader (as opposed to simply listening or even sleeping!). As the family of God, we bring our concerns, our fears, our joys, and our hopes both for ourselves and for others before a loving God. Just as in the affirmation of faith, our prayers for and with one another symbolize that we can count on the faith community in good times and bad.

At the end of the prayer, we move to the universal Christian prayer, the Lord's Prayer. We say this prayer together, because Jesus instructed us to do so through his disciples. The whole congregation speaks aloud in prayer and joins the universal church (past, present, and future) as we pray as Christ taught us to pray.

The prayers of the people and the Lord's Prayer can occur in many different places in the worship service. Sometimes it is toward the beginning, right after the announcements and sharing of prayer concerns. Many times it is after the reading and proclamation of the Word. Once we have heard God's Word read and proclaimed, we are acutely aware of God's faithfulness and our need to approach God with the things that concern us most.

Most often these prayers are said by a leader. However, it is appropriate to ask for a whole congregation to pray out loud or silently. Sometimes the leader will bid the congregation to pray for certain things and then allow time for the people to pray silently. Sometimes a leader will call for the congregation to call out names or words of concern. Sometimes prayers are expressed through liturgical movement. The Lord's Prayer is often sung in one of the many musical versions that have been written over the years.

Prayer nurtures the core of our relationship with God. We cannot have a relationship with someone without communicating with that person, and so it is with

God. Prayer is speaking to God and listening for God's response. Prayer is the vital piece of the puzzle that connects us with God in an active relationship.

ACTIVITIES

1. Prayer Wall
(20 minutes, art)

Supplies: Newsprint or butcher paper, a large variety of magazines, scissors, glue, tape

Preparation: Tape newsprint or butcher paper to a wall covering enough space for your entire group to make one big collage. At the top of the paper, write, "Oh God, we pray for . . ." or use the salutation your group commonly uses in prayer. Distribute the magazines, scissors, and glue on enough tables for your group to comfortably work. The floor is also a great place.

Directions: Ask the group to gather around the wall. Explain that in Jerusalem, there is a wall of the temple called the Wailing Wall. For centuries, Jews have been bringing their prayers on pieces of paper and stuffing them into the cracks of the wall. Then, they kneel and pray. Explain that the youth are going to make their own prayer wall today.

Invite the participants to browse through the magazines and look for things that they would like to pray for. They can cut out pictures, headlines, or entire articles. The pictures can symbolize things they want to pray for or be an actual event or situation. Ask them to glue their clippings to the wall when they are ready.

Tell participants to sit in front of the wall when they finish and look at what everyone else is adding. After everyone has finished, divide the group into smaller groups of two or three people. Ask the participants to share what they added to the wall and why.

Next, invite group members to stand facing the prayer wall and to pray silently for what they see. After a few moments of silence, lead the group in the Lord's Prayer by saying, "Now let us pray the prayer that Jesus taught us to pray."

2. Wailing Wall
(20 minutes, meditation)

Supplies: Newsprint or butcher paper, sticky notes (five to ten for each participant), pens/pencils, markers, CD/tape player, quiet instrumental music

Preparation: Tape newsprint or butcher paper on a wall in six columns. (This will serve as the group's "wailing wall.") At the top of the first column, write "Prayers for Me." Title the second column "Prayers for my Family"; the third, "Prayers for My Church"; the fourth, "Prayers for My School"; the fifth, "Prayers for My Community and Country"; and the sixth, "Prayers for the World."

Directions: Invite the participants to gather in front of the "wailing wall." Remind the youth that in Jerusalem there is a wall of the temple called the Wailing Wall.

For centuries, Jews have been bringing their prayers on pieces of paper and stuffing them into the cracks of the wall. Then, they kneel and pray.

Distribute sticky notes and pens/pencils to the participants. Each participant should get several sticky notes. Put the extra sticky notes in a place where participants can easily get more if they need them. Ask the group to look at the categories, write prayers, and post them on the wall in the appropriate categories. Remind the participants that a prayer can be a paragraph, a sentence, a phrase, or even one word. The prayers are for God, so participants should express their prayers as they want. God will understand. Encourage each participant to write at least one prayer for each category.

After about fifteen minutes, ask the group to gather in front of the wailing wall. Remind the group that the power of being in community is that we can pray for one another. We are not just one person praying alone in isolation. We are part of a community of support and faith who lifts one another's prayers to God.

Invite the youth to pray by reading aloud and silently the prayers that have been written on the wall. They do not have to read their own. Tell them that it is okay if they speak over one another while praying. Begin the prayer by saying, "Creator God, we pray for . . ."

This activity may also be set up as a project to use over the course of time at a retreat or even just as a constant prayer tool in a youth room or Sunday school class.

This activity was adapted from Carl Horton's Spirituality Center at the Presbyterian Youth Connection Assembly 2000.

3. Prayer Request Boxes
(45–60 minutes, art)

Supplies: Shoe boxes (one for each prayer box your group plans to make), paint, brushes, paint supplies, construction paper, other collage materials, tape, prayer-request forms, hole punch, string, pens

Preparation: Place one shoe box on each table with a set of paints and other collage supplies. Make copies of the prayer-request forms.

Directions: This activity is excellent to do at the beginning of a retreat so that prayer requests can be collected and prayed for during the retreat. However, the youth can also use this activity as an ongoing project for their church and community.

First, review the introduction to this chapter. Invite the young people to consider who will use the prayer-request boxes and where they will be placed. Remind them that they are committing to pray for the requests in the boxes, so they should commit to do something that they really can do. It might be a great idea to put them all over your town, but people will have to commit to managing the pickup, maintenance, and prayers of the boxes. If the youth are considering placing them at their schools, check with your local school administration about the possibilities.

Ask participants to paint and decorate the boxes. They can be as creative as they want as long as it is clear that the boxes are prayer-request boxes. If the boxes will be placed outside your church or retreat setting, include an identification note on the box that displays your group's name and the pledge to pray for the requests placed in the box.

Cut a slit in the top of the box to insert prayer requests. Attach the pen to the box by tying a string to the pen, and then punch two holes in the box where you can tie the other end of the string. Attach the prayer-request forms to the box as well by punching a hole in the upper corner of each request form. Tie them onto the string, and then tie the string to the box.

Make arrangements for the boxes to be distributed to the chosen locations. Also, decide who will pick up the prayer requests and when. Decide how and when you will pray for the requests.

Close the session by praying that the boxes may be a sign of God's light in the world, that your group might faithfully follow through with the commitment to pray for others, and that people who need to be prayed for will find the boxes and be bold enough to request prayer.

4. Labyrinth
(30–60 minutes, meditation and movement)

Supplies: A labyrinth, candles, CD/tape player, soft instrumental music

Directions: The labyrinth is an excellent spiritual practice of prayer. Participants walk a circular path into the center of the labyrinth design. As they walk, they engage in prayer and reflection. After more prayer and reflection on the inside of the circle, participants walk prayerfully back out of the labyrinth. The labyrinth is a flexible tool that can be used for any kind of prayer in any kind of way. It can serve as a prayer of the people as the participants take the labyrinth journey and pray for themselves, their community of faith, and the world. See http://www.labyrinthproject.com for information on using the labyrinth, making a labyrinth, or ordering one.

5. Newspaper Prayer
(15–20 minutes, discussion)

Supplies: Current newspapers (preferably from the day you do the activity), scissors, paper, pens/pencils

Directions: Invite the group to browse through the newspapers. Ask the participants to cut out headlines of articles or issues that concern them. Encourage each person to cut at least three headlines.

After everyone has finished, place the headlines on the floor or a table so that everyone can see them. Ask the group to put them into categories. Possible categories are politics, world issues, local community, or school and youth. After the clippings have been put into categories, divide the group into as many smaller groups as there are categories. Give each group paper, pens/pencils, and a set of clippings. Ask the groups to write a prayer using the headlines they have been given as their subject.

After the groups have finished, gather in the circle and pray the prayers that have been written. End the session by saying the Lord's Prayer together.

Prayer Request Form

This prayer request form is being provided

By

_____

(church or group name)

We commit to

pray confidentially and faithfully

for your concern.

Prayer Request:

Name (optional):

6. The Lord's Prayer in Music
(10–30 minutes, music and reflection)

Supplies: CD/tape player, several different musical versions of the Lord's Prayer, copies of the discussion questions, paper, pens/pencils, newsprint, markers, tape

Preparation: Ask participants in your group to bring versions of the Lord's Prayer that they may have in their own music collections. Also, we suggest Charlotte Church's *Voice of an Angel*; the *Sarafina!* soundtrack; Art Garfunkel's *Songs from a Parent to a Child*; and Cliff Richard's *The Millennium Prayer*. You may also have people in your group who play an instrument or sing and who would be willing to share a version with the group.

Note: When using the *Sarafina!* version, please be aware that it has been recorded in the context of a movie and at the very end, there is some dialogue where an inappropriate word is used. If you turn off the music when you hear the young people cheering at the end, you will avoid it.

Directions: There are two ways to use this activity. First, simply play the different versions of the Lord's Prayer during worship. Ask participants to meditate and pray the Lord's Prayer as they listen. The other way is to use the music for discussion.

Begin by reading aloud in the group Matthew 6:9–13. Distribute the discussion questions, pens/pencils, and paper. Invite the participants to write their reflections as they listen to each version.

After you have played the different musical versions of the prayer, ask the following: Name all the versions presented (make a list and tape it on the wall for participants to see). Which version inspired you? Which version bored you? Next, use the discussion questions for further discussion. Afterward, pray aloud together the Lord's Prayer.

Discussion Questions:
1. What kind of music is this?
2. What does the music emphasize or say about the prayer?
3. Why do you think somebody would record a version of the prayer like this?
4. What are you feeling as you listen to the song?
5. What are you thinking as you listen to the song?
6. What did you learn about the Lord's Prayer by listening to this version of it?

7. Lord's Prayer Sculptures
(20 minutes, liturgical movement)

Supplies: Bibles or copies of Matthew 6:9–13

Directions: Read Matthew 6:9–13 aloud in the group. Then, divide the group into five smaller groups of three to five people. If your group is smaller than ten, divide into two smaller groups and give each group more than one Scripture sculpture assignment. If your group is larger than twenty-five, give some groups the same Scripture sculpture assignment.

Assign each group a different part of the Lord's Prayer (v. 9, v. 10, v. 11, v. 12, v. 13). Invite the groups to create a sculpture that represents their verse. The sculpture must consist of every person in the group and not include movement. Give the groups ten minutes to create their sculptures.

Gather the groups together and invite them to share their sculptures in order of the verses. Or you may ask them to share their sculptures while the rest of the group guesses which verse they represent. If you are using this activity outside the worship setting, allow time between each group for others to ask questions, make comments, and show their appreciation.

8. Bidding Prayer
(5–10 minutes, prayer and meditation)

Supplies: Copy of the Lord's Prayer, the Prayer of Francis of Assisi (can be found in *The Book of Common Worship*, p. 25), or a list of categories or general subjects for prayer

Directions: Explain to the group that a bidding prayer is one in which the leader uses a general outline to direct the congregation to pray for certain things. For example, the leader may say, "Let us pray for our country." Then, the participants would pray silently or out loud for the country.

You may create your own list of general subjects or you may ask your group to create a list before praying. You may also use the Lord's Prayer as a guide. Stop after each verse and allow time for prayer. Ask the participants to use each line of the prayer to guide their prayer. Remind them that a "prayer of the people" is not solely for themselves but also a time to intercede on the behalf of others.

The Prayer of Francis of Assisi is also excellent to use as a bidding prayer. After each line of the prayer, allow time for silent and spoken prayer. This prayer develops from an inward thinking about self to an outward thinking about the world and those around us.

9. Prayer Collage
(15–30 minutes, art)

Supplies: Construction paper, glue, scissors, markers, crayons, magazines, fabric scraps, other collage supplies

Directions: Ask each participant to pick a piece of construction paper. Distribute pens/pencils and invite participants to make a list of people or situations that need prayer. Ask them not to think in generalities but in terms of their personal concerns and situations. Then, ask them to turn over their paper and make a collage prayer on the other side. A collage prayer is a visual prayer. The collage should represent who and what they are praying for. It should also represent what they are asking God to do (God's will, understanding, healing, love, etc.).

After the participants have finished, ask them to place their collages in the middle of the circle. Ask them to quietly view all of the collages. At this point, the youth may pray for what they see or discuss the following questions. End the discussion in prayer, using the collages as the guide.

Discussion Questions:

1. What common elements are in the collages?
2. What unique elements are in the collages?
3. Who are we praying for?
4. What are we asking God to do?

10. Prayer Journalism
(time is dependent on choices made for activity, discussion)

Supplies: Paper, pens/pencils, copies of the interview questions

Directions: Gather your group and invite the youth to play the role of journalists writing a story on prayer. Their story must consist of prayer requests from the community around them. Divide your group into pairs and ask them to go out on interviews. The pairs can take turns asking the questions and writing down the answers. The "journalists" should thank every person they interview for their time and explain that they will be praying for their requests when they return to the group.

If you use this activity in a retreat setting, ask the journalists to interview those who are also attending the retreat. The youth can use this activity in your church and interview other church members, or interview people in their school or community.

In this age of technology, you may choose for your group to videotape the interviews. Ask each pair to choose and share some of the highlights of their interviews. You may also find a computer expert in your group who can edit the videos.

After the interviews are complete, gather your group and discuss the following:

1. How did it feel to be a journalist?
2. How did people react to your questions?
3. What common themes appeared in the interviews?
4. What unique requests did you receive?

Next, ask the pairs to write a prayer that includes all the requests they received. Tell them to be specific when specific names or situations appear. After the participants have written their prayers, pray them together using the Lord's Prayer to conclude.

Interview Questions:

1. If you could ask God for one thing, what would it be?
2. If you were to pray for one person right now, who would it be?
3. If you were to pray for one situation in life, what would it be?

WORKS CITED

The Theology and Worship Ministry Unit, *Book of Common Worship.* 1993. Louisville, Ky.: Westminster/John Knox Press.

CHAPTER 9

Offering

The offering is a response to God's goodness. It is important to remember that a basic Reformed Christian belief is that God always acts first. Thus, we must never become arrogant about how much money, time, or talent we are giving to God through the church or other activities. Jesus instructs us in Matthew by saying, "You received without payment; give without payment" (10:8b). We must always remember that God has given us everything we have and that we are blessed to be able to give something back.

The offering is a time when the money goes into the plate, but it is also a time to reflect on how we might respond to God's goodness through our actions. Hebrews 13:16 says, "Do not neglect to do good and to share what you have, for such sacrifices are pleasing to God." In church worship services, it is easy to focus on the monetary aspect of giving as we watch the plates being passed, but the offering is so much more than that. God's work is done through the use of our talents. It is done through our devotion of time to a certain project that needs help. God's work is accomplished by the way we behave toward others in the world around us. Remember that the offering is always more than money. It is a response to God's gifts with our whole lives.

ACTIVITIES

1. Scavenger Hunt
(20 minutes, game)

Supplies: Copies of the scavenger hunt list; rope, tape, or cones to make a boundary area

Preparation: Designate a boundary area that is big enough to comfortably hold your group, plus a little more room. The youth should be able to walk or run around the space. Hide the items on the scavenger hunt list throughout the boundary area. (See the list on p. 90.)

Directions: Distribute the scavenger hunt lists. Tell the participants they have five minutes to find as many items as they can on the list. There is only one rule: They may not leave the boundary area to find these things. When participants find the items, they should place them in the middle of the boundary area. After the time is up, ask the youth to count how many things they found. Congratulate them on their success.

Now explain to the group that when we give to God, we give only what we have. We don't give what we wish we could give or what we might have tomorrow. We give what we have now. We give what we have within the boundaries of our resources, and that is good enough.

Invite the youth to look at the pile of stuff they have collected. Ask them to find one thing that symbolizes what they want to give to God. Remind the participants to think about what it is they have and what they really can give. Explain that they shouldn't think in hypotheticals but in real-life specifics. Someone might say, "I choose a penny because I'm going to start giving 10 percent of my baby-sitting money to the offering," or "I choose a bandage because I want to devote more of my time to helping others with their problems."

If participants cannot find something that truly symbolizes what they wish to give, then let them pick something off the list that was not found or find something in the area that symbolizes their gift.

After everyone has found his or her gift, ask the youth to share their offerings with God by showing the item they picked and telling why they chose it.

2. Thank-you Notes
(20 minutes, art)

Supplies: Blank cards and envelopes, markers, crayons, construction paper, stickers, other art supplies to decorate the cards, newsprint, tape, markers

Directions: Ask the group to brainstorm the definition of "blessing." Write the definitions on a piece of newsprint. Next, ask the participants to call out all the people who have blessed them over their lifetime. Write their answers on newsprint. Finally, ask them to brainstorm how God has blessed them over their lifetime. Write their answers on the newsprint.

Give each participant a card and envelope. Ask the youth to write a thank-you note to one of the people they listed on the newsprint. They may decorate the front in any way that visually expresses the blessing they received from the person they are thanking. Remind them that they may also include Scripture (see the Psalms for many words of thanksgiving). Help the participants make arrangements to mail the cards.

Next, give each participant another card and envelope. This time, ask the participants to choose one blessing God has given them. They should decorate the card so that it represents the blessing. Invite them to write a thank-you note or prayer of thanksgiving to God on the inside of the card. Then, ask them to write how they will respond to God's blessing. What will be their offering to God? After the participants have finished, ask them to seal the card in the envelope. Tell them to write their name on the outside (where their address would go).

Scavenger Hunt List

Find these things on people in your group or in the assigned area.

A sandal	A feather
7 pieces of pocket lint	A forked stick
A watch	A piece of trash
A broken watch	A penny
A shoelace	A driver's license
A pencil	A bandage
Socks with stripes	A bookmark
A Bible	Anything with a cartoon character on it
A button	Anything with a Christian symbol on it
A safety pin	A portable CD or tape player
A gold earring	A personal digital assistant (PDA)
A tennis shoe	A tube of lipstick
A hair tie, bow, or "scrunchy"	A baseball cap
A key	A set of keys
A toy	A picture of someone's family
A rock	A piece of gum
A leaf	

During worship, invite the youth to place their cards in the offering baskets when it is time. Tell the participants that in one month, they will receive their cards in the mail to be reminded of God's blessing and their commitment. Make arrangements for a participant to mail the cards in one month.

3. Offering Aerobics
(10 minutes, game)

Directions: Invite the youth to stand in a circle. Instruct them to think of an offering that they can give to God. Encourage the participants to think of something real that they have to offer. Ask them to think in terms of gifts that they have and how they could use those gifts in their faith life (such as playing piano, making a quilt for someone, listening to their friends, or bowling in a bowl-a-thon for charity). After the youth have chosen their offering, ask them to think of a sign or motion they can make to represent their offering. Someone might make a big smile; another individual might point to his or her ear; another might pretend to be playing piano or bowling.

Start with yourself. Say, "Hi! My name is _____. I will give God _____." Then make your sign. Instruct the group to respond to you by saying your name and making the same sign you made. Then, ask the person to your left to go next. After each group member has said his or her name and made the sign, go back to your name and sign. Keep going around the circle with everyone repeating the participants' names and signs sequentially together.

After you have completed the circle, ask everyone to find a new place in the circle. See if you can go around the circle and repeat the names and signs. Invite individuals to see if they can go all the way around the circle naming people and their offerings. Conclude the game with a prayer asking God to bless the offerings and help the participants stay committed to their faith and response to God.

4. Offering ABCs
(5 minutes, game)

Directions: Gather the group in a circle. Tell the youth that they will go around the circle and call out blessings that God has given them. The only trick is that they will do it alphabetically. Start with yourself and call out a blessing that begins with "a." The next person should call out a blessing that begins with "b," and so on.

After you have completed the alphabet, ask the youth to think of things they could give back to God or ways they could respond to God's blessings. Pick a new place to start in the circle and go through the alphabet as before. At the end, say, "And all the people said, 'Amen!' "

5. Prayer of Francis of Assisi
(20–30 minutes, movement/discussion)

Supplies: Copies of the Prayer of Francis of Assisi (which can be found in the *Book of Common Worship*, p. 25), pens/pencils

Directions: If you have a large group, divide your group into smaller groups of four to six people. If you are a group of eight or less, do this activity as one group. Ask the group(s) to stand in a circle facing one another. Tell the youth that you will read a list of words. For each word you read, they are to form a sculpture with their bodies as one group. The sculpture should be still. The youth may not talk as they move into their sculpture, and they must be touching one another. They should move from one sculpture to another.

Here is the list of words: hate, love, injury, pardon, doubt, faith, despair, hope, darkness, light, sadness, joy. Go through the words a couple of times until the group can easily move from one to the other. It is OK if the sculptures come out differently each time. At this point, tell the youth you are going to read a prayer that contains the words. Ask them to face one another and move to the words as you read them in the context of the prayer of Francis of Assisi. Pause after each movement word to give the participants time to move. If you have a large group, ask the smaller groups to share their sculptures with one another as you read the prayer again.

Afterwards, distribute a copy of the prayer to each person and ask the participants to discuss the following questions:

1. How did you feel while doing the sculptures?
2. Which sculpture was especially moving, invoked the most thought, or was more powerful for you than the others?
3. Which one of these tasks is the hardest for you: to be loving, to forgive, to be faithful, to have hope, to live in light, or to experience joy? Which one is the easiest?
4. Which task is the hardest for the people around you (school, friends, family, church, society, etc.)? Which one is the easiest?

Next, ask the youth to look at the second half of the prayer. For every line of the second half, ask them to respond to the following questions and write their answers next to the corresponding line:

1. Who can you console?
2. Who needs understanding from you?
3. Who needs love from you?
4. What can you give to God in response to God's goodness to you?
5. Who do you need to forgive?
6. What does eternal life mean to you?

Divide the group into pairs and ask them to share their answers. Tell them they can share as much or as little as they would like. After discussion, ask participants to fold their papers so that they can put them in the offering basket during worship.

6. Offering Banners
(60 minutes, Bible study/art)

Supplies: Bibles, copies of the discussion questions, sheets or large pieces of canvas cut into four-by-four-foot squares to make up to six banners (size is dependent on the size of the group), several different colors of paints (tempera or acrylic), brushes, water, paper towels, drop cloths, cleanup supplies. (You can also use newsprint or butcher paper with markers, crayons, fabric scraps, construction paper, and other collage supplies.)

Preparation: Place the blank banners far enough apart so that each group may comfortably work around its banner. Be sure to put drop cloths under each banner (especially if you are working on the floor). Distribute the banner-making supplies.

Directions: Divide your group into smaller groups of two or three people. Give each group a Bible and assign each one of the following Scripture verses: Psalm 24:1; Matthew 10:8b; 2 Corinthians 9:6; 2 Corinthians 9:7; Hebrews 13:16; or Acts 20:35b. Ask the youth to read their passage aloud in the group. Then, discuss the following questions:

Discussion Questions:

1. What is the passage telling us to do?
2. Why are we supposed to give?
3. What is our motivation for giving?
4. How does this Scripture compare to how you usually feel about the offering?
5. Is it reflective of how our church approaches offering?

After discussion, assign each group a banner area. Ask the youth to make a banner that symbolizes their Scripture verse. After the banners are completed, invite the entire group to go on a banner tour. Stand around each banner and listen to the smaller group's Scripture verse and explanation of its banner. Allow time for others to make comments, ask questions, and show their appreciation.

After the banner tour, discuss the following questions as a group:

1. What common elements are in the Scripture verses and banners? (How are they the same?)
2. What unique elements are in the Scripture verses and banners? (How are they different?)
3. Considering all the verses, what should our motivation be for giving to God?
4. What should we give to God?

7. Taking Inventory
(25 minutes, discussion)

Supplies: Copies of the inventory sheets, pens/pencils, Bibles

Directions: In the whole group, read aloud the following Scriptures: Psalm 24:1; Matthew 10:8b; 2 Corinthians 9:6; 2 Corinithians 9:7; Hebrews 13:16; and Acts 20:35b. After each Scripture reading, discuss the following questions:

1. What is the passage telling us to do?
2. Why are we supposed to give?
3. What is our motivation for giving?
4. How does this Scripture compare to how you usually feel about the offering?

Next, pass out the inventory sheets and invite participants to complete them. Explain that an inventory list is an accounting of all that a person has. Often we see a store taking inventory (or account) of all the items on its shelves. This inventory list is a personal inventory list of all we have to give to God. Instruct participants to write down things they actually have and can actually do.

After the participants have completed the inventories, invite them to share with the whole group, or you can divide the group into smaller groups of two to three for sharing. After the sharing, ask the participants to fold their papers so that they can put them in the offering basket during worship.

WORKS CITED

The Theology and Worship Ministry Unit, *Book of Common Worship*. 1993. Louisville, Ky.: Westminster/John Knox Press.

Inventory List

What gifts and talents do I have? (everything from kindness to playing the piano)

How can I use these gifts and talents in response to God's goodness in my life?

What can I do that requires physical labor?

How much money do I have and how much can I give?

How can I overcome any obstacles that might stop me from doing the above?

CHAPTER 10

The Charge and Benediction

The charge and benediction are given at the very end of the service. They are usually followed only by a response sung by the congregation or the choir and perhaps the playing of a postlude (on the organ or other instrument) while people leave the worship space.

The charge and benediction function as the close of the service, but they also function as the beginning of our life lived as Christians in the world. We described the call to worship as a starting line or the beginning. The charge and benediction may seem like the end or close of one thing, but the intention is that they serve as another "starting line" or "beginning." In the charge and benediction, God says to us, "Go!" and tells us how we should go. It is the time when we are given a command to follow the Word of God out of the church.

Often the charge is directly related to the message of the service. It consists of a few short sentences that reiterate the call to action expressed earlier in the sermon or Scripture reading. Empowered by the Holy Spirit, we are given direction to be examples of Christ in the world and to live in his name. Often, we are charged with a new task, a new way to live, or a new way to think. The charge can come in the form of quoted Scripture, a few sentences from the sermon, a song, a drama, or liturgical movement.

The benediction is the blessing that follows the charge. The blessing assures us that God goes with us on our way as we seek to live our faith in the world. According to Reformed tradition, the benediction should use Trinitarian language. In other words, we go in the name of the Creator, Redeemer, and Sustainer or Father, Son, and Holy Spirit. The blessing or the benediction is to be one that gives the assurance of God's constant presence in our lives.

ACTIVITIES

1. Mission: Impossible
(20 minutes, discussion)

Supplies: TV, VCR, videotape of the *Mission: Impossible* movie with Tom Cruise, index cards (one for each participant), pens/pencils

Preparation: Write "Charge" on half of the index cards; on the other half, write "Blessing." Fast-forward the videotape to the scene where the Tom Cruise character receives his initial mission. The scene takes place at the beginning of the movie when he is in an airplane. The end of the clip comes when his tape smolders in the player.

Directions: Gather the group around the TV/VCR. Tell the youth you are going to show them a video where a person receives a charge. In other words, this person gets some directions on what they are supposed to do. Show the video clip to the group.

   After the video, divide the group into smaller groups of three people and discuss the following questions:

   1. How did the message (or charge) come to him?
   2. Was the message (or charge) clear?
   3. How did it make him feel?
   4. Was there a promise that went with the charge?
   5. How would you feel if you were him?
   6. Would you have done it? Why or why not?
   7. How are God's charges to us the same as the one Tom Cruise got?
   8. How are God's charges different than this one?
   9. What difference does it make that God's charges always come with a blessing?

After the discussion is concluded, invite the smaller groups to return to the larger group and share the highlights of their discussion. Then, give half the participants "Charge" index cards and the other half "Blessing" index cards. Hand out pens/pencils and ask the participants to write either a charge or a blessing on their index card.

   Next, ask the charge people to stand in one line and the blessing people to stand in another. The lines should face each other so that each charge person is looking at a blessing person. Ask the participants to take turns going down the line, saying their blessing and/or charge to the person across from them. Start with the first person in the charge line, and then go to the first person in the blessing line. Continue until everyone has a turn. Then, ask the youth to shout "Amen!" when they have finished.

2. Bible Benedictions
(10–15 minutes, discussion/writing)

Supplies: Bibles, pens/pencils, paper, newsprint, markers

Preparation: Choose several of Paul's benedictions from his letters. Some options are Romans 16:25–27; 1 Corinthians 16:21–24; 2 Corinthians 13:11–14; Galatians 6:14–16; Ephesians 6:23–24; Philippians 4:21–23, 1 Thessalonians 5:23–28; 2 Thessalonians 3:16; Hebrews 13:20–21; or 2 Peter 3:18.

Write the biblical reference on a piece of newsprint or a chalkboard. You may also need to study the Scripture beforehand so that you may provide some background information to the youth when they look at the questions below. Look for commentaries in your church or local library, or ask your pastor, youth minister, or educator for help.

Directions: Distribute the Bibles, paper, and pens/pencils. Divide the young people into small groups of two to four persons and assign them a passage to read. Ask them to discuss the following in their small groups:

1. Who was the letter written to?
2. What situation was the writer in when he wrote the letter?
3. What situation was the church or group of people in as they read the letter?
4. How does this Scripture passage and the situation of the people in it relate to your life?
5. How does this Scripture passage and the situation of the people in it relate to our group?

Next, ask the small groups to write down all the action words (verbs) of their Scripture passage in a column on the paper. Invite the small groups to write a charge to the larger group using the action words from their Scripture passage. Gather the groups into a circle and invite them to read aloud to the other group members.

3. Charge and Blessing for the Church
(10 minutes, discussion)

Supplies: Four or five sheets of newsprint or chalkboard, markers

Directions: Ask the group to think about all the things the church does. List the responses on a piece of newsprint. Encourage them to think about all aspects of the church's ministry to the congregation, community, and missions.

Next, divide the group into four small groups. Give each group four areas of ministry from the list so that each group has different ministries from all the other groups. Ask the groups to list their four assigned ministries on the newsprint and then write a positive, uplifting sentence of direction or blessing for the first ministry on their paper.

Rotate the papers by passing each newsprint sheet to another group. Now ask the groups to write a statement for the second ministry listed on the sheet. Continue rotating the sheet until all four ministries have a statement.

Gather together and write the ministries and the charge statements on one sheet of paper or a chalkboard. Encourage the participants to decorate the sheets with pictures and symbols. Discuss the following questions:

1. From the charges and blessings that you wrote to the different ministries of the church, pick out one that applies to you. Why does it apply to you?
2. Pick out one that applies to our group. Why does it apply?
3. How do you support or carry out the ministries of the church?
4. How can we participate more in the life of these ministries and the church?

When everyone has finished, invite the group to stand and read the list of charges and blessings together.

4. The Church's Mission Statement
(30 minutes, discussion and optional liturgical movement)

Supplies: Copies of your church's mission statement, pencils, markers, paper, Bibles

Directions: Many churches have a mission statement they print in their bulletins or newsletters or keep in their records. In this activity the young people will explore their church's mission statement, discuss its main emphasis, and write a charge to the church.

Gather your group and distribute copies of your church's mission statement. Read the statement together. Discuss the following:

1. What is the focus of the church?
2. To whom do we seek to minister?
3. What is our main mission?
4. How does the church wish to carry out the mission?
5. How is the church currently living its mission?
6. If you could add anything, what would you add?

Now ask the group to create a charge and blessing based on the church's mission statement. Tell the youth to think of the charge and blessing as a reminder of the mission and a message of encouragement. The message should be a few short lines. They may choose to include lines from a Scripture passage, or perhaps a familiar benediction they have heard before. They may write the message using their own youth vernacular. Encourage them to be creative and make the message their own. After they have finished, ask them to stand together and read their charge and blessing out loud.

Another option is to create movements to go with the church's mission statement. Depending on the number of sentences or phrases in the statement, divide the participants into that many groups. Give each group one phrase or sentence from the statement. Have the groups create movements that describe their sentence. The simpler the movements, the more effective the message will be. Ask them to choose one person as the reader while the rest do the movements. After they have finished, ask each group to share their liturgical movement creation with the others.

If the youth are new to doing movement or they're having trouble developing ideas, suggest they use a sign-language handbook. Try *The Joy of Signing* by Lottie L. Riekehof. It is especially helpful because it includes religious words. (See the Works Cited at the end of this book.)

5. Moving Benediction
(30 minutes, liturgical movement)

Supplies: Copies of a common charge/benediction your church or group uses

Directions: Invite the young people to read a common charge/benediction that is used in your church. Discuss the following:

1. What are we being told to do?
2. Who are we being called to be?
3. What blessing are we being given?

Next, ask the young people to think of ways they could act out the words. Invite them to create a liturgical movement piece based on the charge/benediction they have discussed. Encourage them to begin by looking at the action words of the statement. The youth should act out those words based on the way they are described in the statement.

Another option is to break your large group into groups of four to eight people. Give each group one phrase or sentence from the charge/benediction. Ask them to work together to create a frozen sculpture that represents their phrase or sentence.

Finally, read the benediction aloud and have the groups present their movements.

6. Benedict a Friend
(2 minutes, activity)

Supplies: A copy of the following benediction or one you or the group has written:

> (Say the name of your partner.)
> You are a child of God.
> God loves you.
> Christ died for your sins, so you can be free.
> The Holy Spirit will be your guide.
> Go in peace.
> Amen.

Directions: This activity is a good benediction for a closing worship at the end of a retreat. It is also helpful in the commissioning of a large group as they go to perform a particular task or mission.

Ask the young people in your group to find a partner. The partners should face each other. Invite them to hold hands or put a hand on each other's shoulder. Tell them to make sure they know their partner's name. Ask the members of the group to repeat after you the chosen benediction. They should keep looking at their partner as they speak.

7. Benediction Songs
(5 minutes, discussion)

Supplies: Copies of the lyrics of songs (already recorded or to be sung) that include messages of being sent out or being blessed

Music Resources: *The Presbyterian Hymnal, New Song* songbook, *Songs and Creations*

Suggested Recorded Songs: "I Will Go" by S.G.G.L. (*Going South*); "We Are Each Other's Angels" by Chuck Brodsky (sung by David Lamotte on *Flying*); "Step by Step" (sung by Whitney Houston on *The Preacher's Wife* soundtrack)

Directions: Gather the young people to sing and/or listen to a song that has messages of sending out. Pass out copies of the lyrics to the chosen song. Invite the youth to circle the words or phrases that stand out to them as they sing or listen to the song. Discuss the following:

1. What charge or blessing is the song giving us?
2. What words or phrases stood out to you? Why?

Ask them to sing or listen to the song one more time as closure to worship.

Another option is to invite the group to create a liturgical movement piece to the song to use in a future worship service.

8. Benediction Chant
(20 minutes, game)

Supplies: Paper, pens/pencils, newsprint, tape, a marker, a Scripture reading, song lyrics, or other writing to be used for the benediction (percussion instruments are recommended but optional)

Directions: Follow the instructions for the Word Chant activity on page 49 of chapter 5, but use a benediction. Repeat the chant a few times in the worship space and then keep repeating and keeping the beat as the worship service concludes.

9. Open Doors
(5–15 minutes, meditation)

Supplies: Worship space where the doors or windows can be opened to hear the sounds of the world outside

Preparation: Make sure the doors or windows can be easily opened and have someone stationed to do the opening.

Directions: Before the charge/benediction is read, open the doors and windows. Ask the participants to listen closely for what they hear outside. After a few minutes, ask them to be aware of their thoughts and feelings as they prepare to go out into the world they hear. Then, ask a young person in the group to read the charge and benediction. Be sure to allow several minutes for meditation and listening.

Discussion Questions: Use the following questions to discuss the meditation:

1. What worldly noises did you hear?
2. What were you thinking or feeling?
3. Did you feel a sense of urgency to go out?
4. Is there a comfort about being in the worship space that makes you want to stay?
5. How did the words of the charge and benediction encourage you in your leaving?

10. Transitions
(10 minutes, art)

Supplies: Play-Doh, two pieces of newsprint, markers, chalkboard

Directions: Since the charge/benediction is the conclusion of worship, it is easy to think of it as a stopping point. Actually, it is a pivotal point in the life of a Christian. The charge/benediction is the transition where God sends us from the sanctuary of worship out into the world to do God's will. Many young people focus on transitions with joy and expectation, but some transitions can be difficult. This activity is an opportunity for young people to reflect on the transitional experiences they have had and to discuss possible future transitions.

Ask the participants to call out all the significant transitions (both positive and negative) they have been through in their life. List their responses on one side of the newsprint. Then, ask the youth to call out all the transitions they are anticipating for the future and list the responses on the other side of the newsprint. Some examples of transitions are moving to a new house or city; beginning elementary school, middle school, or high school; a death; a divorce; breakups of relationships; changes of friends; going through confirmation class; starting in youth group; the first time at a retreat; learning to drive; or a first date.

Next, give each person some Play-Doh. Ask the participants to reflect on the transitions that have been discussed. Ask them to make two sculptures: one for the most significant transition of their past and one for the most significant transition they think they will have in the future.

After the participants have finished, invite them to gather in groups of three. Ask them to show one another their transition sculptures and share why they are significant. Tell the participants that if they do not wish to share, they can simply show their sculpture and not explain it. They only have to share what they want.

Next, gather the smaller groups back into the large group and ask the participants to share highlights from their smaller groups. Ask them to identify the similarities and differences between one another's sculptures.

After the discussion, invite the participants to put their sculptures on a sheet of newsprint or cardboard in the center of the group. Ask them to stand in a circle around the sculptures. Read a charge and benediction to the group. This may serve as the end of worship. If you are using this activity in an educational format, discuss the following question: How do the charge and benediction help to prepare you for the transitions in life?

11. Basket Weave Prayer
(5 minutes, game)

Directions: Follow the directions for the Basket Weave Prayer activity on page 23 of chapter 2. After the group is standing inside the circle, explain how the circle is like God's family. The youth have been called to worship, have worshiped together, and now are being called to leave this circle so that they might live their faith in the world. However, the circle always exists as our community of faith. It will always be here as a place of refuge, support, and strength.

Ask participants to think of one word that expresses something that they are thankful for concerning the group and one word that expresses a hope they have as they leave. For example, someone might say, "I am thankful for friends. I hope for peace." Invite participants to share after you open the prayer. End by asking everyone to say "Amen."

CHAPTER 11

Music

Throughout Judeo-Christian history, music has played a vital role in worship. From the Psalms of the Old Testament to Paul's exhortation that we "sing psalms and hymns and spiritual songs" (Eph. 5:19), the Scripture affirms music's integral role in worship from beginning to end. We use music not simply to transition from one worship element to another, to entertain the congregation, or to cover silence in a worship service. We use music to express worship elements themselves. We communicate our faith in God and express our love for God through music. We pray through music. We proclaim God's Word through music.

Music was an important part of the Reformation and representative of the shift from a worship service that excluded the congregation to a worship service where the congregation became an important part of the liturgy. First, worship incorporated congregational hymns, songs, and choruses. Second, the music was translated into the people's language, allowing them to participate fully. Third, the music assimilated the culture and daily life of the time by using new lyrics to old tunes—even old tavern tunes.

Over the last several decades, there has been much talk about diversity of music in worship. Various musical styles have developed in our sanctuaries that add to the traditional and classical forms. These include praise music, jazz, contemporary Christian, rhythmic, and others. The PC(USA) and other denominations continue to discern how to balance traditional music styles and needs with the newer styles. Some congregations have chosen a "blended" model of worship. Others use two services with different music styles for each. The fact that the style of worship is often characterized by the style of music used points to the importance of music in worship.

The best way to study music in worship is to join in and sing or play. Some groups have a long history of singing and praising God together through music. Other youth would rather be rolled in thumbtacks before they would join in a group singing time! You may determine that a small group of youth in your church would enjoy music activities together instead of with the whole group—and that is OK. You have to start somewhere. Find out who in your group plays an instrument in the school band or orchestra. Who sings in the school choir? Who is known for belting out pop songs in their car to and from school? Test the waters and be ready to adjust to fit the needs of your young people.

You may still study music in worship without having group sing-alongs or developing youth choirs. Invite the music minister to speak, gather a group of interested young people to sing tunes used in worship, or invite choir members to sing. You can also use recorded music.

There are several pieces of music typically used in a Reformed worship service (contemporary or traditional). The Gloria (also known as the Gloria Patri) is right after the assurance of pardon. The two words *Gloria* and *Patri* are translated *Glory* and *Father.* Upon receiving the good news that God has forgiven our sins, we celebrate by giving God glory. Some examples of Glorias can be found in *The Presbyterian Hymnal:* 566, 567, and 575–579. Other Glorias can be found in the *New Song* songbook.

The Doxology is sung right after the offering has been taken. Its function is to give God praise for all the blessings God has given. It emphasizes that our offerings are really God's gifts. Examples of doxologies can be found in *The Presbyterian Hymnal:* 591–593. Other doxologies can be found in the *New Song* songbook.

Other musical elements that are often found in worship include the prelude, an introit, a kyrie, anthems, an offertory, the choral response, and a postlude. In these roles, music is used to help us prepare or meditate upon a certain aspect of worship. Music also can serve as an element of worship itself. We sometimes sing a call to worship, we praise God through an anthem, or we sing a benediction before we leave. Music is an excellent way to worship God. Its uses are endless!

One resource that should be highlighted is the *New Song* songbook. It is an excellent music resource to use with young people. Edited by Beth Watson and published by the PC(USA), this book is a large collection of songs written and used by youth and their leaders throughout the PC(USA) and other denominations. The songs range from very simple to more intricate, with a variety of styles, including several in different languages. One of the best features is an index in the back of the leader's guide that lists songs in categories according to the different elements of Reformed worship—from the call to worship to the benediction. T.E.A.M. highly recommends *New Song* for youth ministers to use both in youth fellowship activities and in congregational worship settings.

The following activities are designed to help youth praise God and also aid in considering how music can be used in worship. You will also find music activities in other chapters of the book.

ACTIVITIES

1. New Words to Old Tunes
(20 minutes, writing/singing)

Supplies: A hymnal for each person, newsprint, markers, an instrumentalist (optional)

Preparation: Choose a list of hymns that are familiar (by tune) to your group. Ask someone to come play the organ, piano, or guitar when you sing the hymns.

Directions: Divide your group into smaller groups of four people. If you are working with young people, it is helpful to have an adult in each group. Distribute the hymnals. Give each group a sheet of newsprint and a marker. Assign each group a different hymn to study. Tell the group to do the following:

1. Read the hymn aloud (or sing it together if you like).
2. Discuss parts of the song that you don't understand or that confuse you.
3. Determine the basic message of the hymn.

Once the participants have finished these assignments, invite them to rewrite the hymn in their own words. In the interest of time you may want to tackle only one verse. If they are moving quickly, have them do all the verses. They should take each verse and put it in their own words using modern language and teenage vernacular. Tell them to try to fit the new words into the meter of the song. It's okay if they don't all follow the same rhyme scheme. Some of the most traditional hymns don't rhyme well either! Ask them to write their verse(s) on a piece of newsprint so that the larger group will be able to read it.

When all the groups have finished at least one verse of their hymn, bring them together into one large group and try singing each of the new hymns.

2. Worship in Music
(30–45 minutes, singing)

Supplies: *New Song* songbooks or transparencies (or a comparable music resource), a music leader, guitar, piano, or any other musical instruments your group usually uses for singing

Directions: There are two ways to do this activity. You can gather your group and together choose songs from the songbook for each element in the worship order. Otherwise, you (or a group of youth) can choose the songs ahead of time. Using the *New Song* songbook index, choose a song from each part of worship. Lead your group through an entire worship service using all music.

Discussion Questions: After worship, discuss the following questions. Remember to make the best of this experience by encouraging participants to speak in specifics and use personal references.

1. What feelings or thoughts did you experience during the worship service?
2. What song was your favorite? Which was your least favorite?
3. How did the use of music enhance or distract from worship?
4. Look at each song. How was it appropriate to use for the element of worship it represented?
5. If you had chosen the songs, is there one you would have really wanted to choose? Which element would it represent?

3. Instrumental Psalm
(15 minutes, game)

Supplies: Newsprint, markers, various simple instruments (rhythm instruments, tambourines, bells, kazoos, etc.)

Preparation: Choose a psalm (recommended choices: Psalm 100, 150, 149, 66:1–4) and write it on the newsprint so that it can be read by the group. In each line of the psalm, choose a key word or phrase and circle it.

Directions: Gather your group around the newsprint. Ask the youth to read the psalm together. Next, ask each participant to pick an instrument. Ask the group to look at all the circled words and choose an instrument that could somehow represent or "sound like" that word. Some instruments may need to be used twice. Each instrument must be used at least once.

Ask the group to read through the psalm again, but this time each instrument holder will read the line in which their instrument is to be played. The instrument is to be played at the circled word or phrase. Read the psalm this way one or two more times. Then have the group read the psalm silently, playing the instruments in the order the corresponding words appear in the psalm.

4. Name That Tune
(30 minutes, game)

Supplies: Hymnals (or the music resource used in your congregation), piano or keyboard, someone to play the hymns

Preparation: Select several hymns that are familiar to your group and used often. Select the hymns using the following categories: Sung Every Week, Advent/ Christmas, Special Days, An Average Sunday. You may also have special times significant to your own congregations, so choose hymns for those times as well. Give the list to your piano player, so that he or she can be prepared. Some examples are:

Sung Every Week

"Glory Be to the Father"	#579*
"Praise God, from Whom All Blessings Flow"	#591

Advent

"O Come, O Come, Emmanuel"	#9
"Come, Thou Long-Expected Jesus"	#2

Christmas

"Silent Night, Holy Night"	#60
"The First Nowell"	#56

Special Days

"Jesus Christ Is Risen Today"	#123
"Were You There?"	#102
"For All the Saints"	#526
*(in *The Presbyterian Hymnal*)	

Directions: Ask the youth if they believe that they are familiar with the music that is used in worship. Tell them that this game will test their knowledge and see what they really know. Present the categories of hymns to the group. Explain that the pianist is going to play two measures of a hymn. It is up to the person in the "hot seat" to guess the hymn. Tell the youth they don't necessarily have to give the exact name of the hymn. They could sing the first line and that would count, too.

Ask for a volunteer to sit in the hot seat and have the pianist play at random a hymn from the category the volunteer picked. If the volunteer guesses the name of the hymn or sings the first line correctly, then he or she chooses the next player. If the volunteer has trouble, the group can guess, too. Whoever guesses correctly gets to choose the next volunteer. Tell the participants that they can always pass. No one will be forced into the hot seat.

If two measures seem to be too easy for your group, make it only one measure. If the youth are having trouble, extend it to four measures. Whenever a hymn is named correctly, invite the whole group to sing one verse of the hymn.

5. Mix and Match Hymns
(20 minutes, singing)

Supplies: Hymnals (or the music resource used in your congregation), piano or keyboard, someone to play the hymns

Preparation: Compile a list of the most familiar hymns of your congregation. Make note of the tune names and meter (found in the center of the heading directly under the title). For example, "Away in a Manger" is "Cradle Song, 11.11.11.11." Using the metrical index (found in the back of *The Presbyterian Hymnal* and listed by tune numbers first, then alphabetically by tune names), find new hymns that fit the same meter. For instance, "Cradle Song" has the same meter as "St. Denio," the tune typically used for "Immortal, Invisible, God Only Wise." It also has the same meter as "How Firm a Foundation."

Directions: Explain to the group that sometimes we can become accustomed to hearing the same old songs done in the same old way. This activity is a way to spice up things and experience an old hymn in a whole new light. For some of your youth, the idea of singing old hymns to the tune of new hymns will sound just as boring. Ask them to indulge you. After you sing a few of these songs to the tune of other less familiar songs, ask them to think of popular tunes that they know (country, rock, pop, favorite praise songs). See if they can fit some of the hymns you have selected into the tunes of their favorite songs.

Distribute the hymnals and ask them to turn to the original hymn. Tell the music readers to pay no attention to the notes. Ask the pianist to play the new tune through once, and then ask the group to sing the hymn to the new tune.

If your group enjoys this kind of activity, have the youth look up some of their favorite hymns and find alternate tunes in which to sing them.

CHAPTER 12

Communion

The sacrament of Communion is one of two sacraments recognized in the PC(USA) and many other Protestant denominations. A sacrament is a "sacred act." The only two sacraments recognized by the PC(USA) are baptism and Communion. These events are considered sacred, because we believe that the Holy Spirit is present in a special way through the waters of baptism and the bread and wine of Communion.

Communion always occurs after the proclamation of the Word, because the Word is why we celebrate Communion. It is in the Scripture where Jesus tells us to celebrate Communion. Our participation in breaking the bread is an active response to the good news we have just heard. Communion, then, is God's Word in action. Sacraments and Scripture are considered inseparable, because they are the Word proclaimed and enacted.

Communion can lead us through a myriad of emotions and realizations. It connects us with important events in our history, defines our present, and gives us energy and direction for the future. During Communion we might experience sadness or joy. Both emotions are appropriate and expected, because we are people who know of Jesus' sacrifice, but we also know of Jesus' resurrection. The Last Supper must have been filled with tension, fear, and sadness. However, when Jesus broke bread with the disciples after he walked on the road to Emmaus with them, they were filled with joy and understanding.

The following activities are designed to

1. Teach the basic elements of the sacrament and their meanings
2. Engage youth in the many facets and dimensions of Communion
3. Enable youth to experience the sacrament in new ways

ACTIVITIES

1. Communion Name Game
(30 minutes, discussion)

Supplies: Newsprint, markers, tape, copies of Sacrament Names

Preparation: Using three newsprint sheets, write in large letters "Communion" at the top of one, "The Lord's Supper" on another, and "The Eucharist" on the third. Tape each sheet on the wall (or floor) in a different part of the room. Put markers beside each sheet.

Directions: Direct the participants' attention to the newsprint sheets. Tell them that all three of these names refer to the same sacrament. Ask the group members to silently think about which of these names is their personal favorite or preferred name for the sacrament. After they have decided, ask participants to stand beside the name they chose. Once everyone is standing beside a newsprint sheet, ask the youth to use the markers to silently write on the newsprint what they think their preferred name means or why they like that name.

After all the participants have had a chance to think and write on their newsprint, ask them to return to the large group. Take the pieces of newsprint and review them with the whole group. Discuss the following questions:

1. What are the common themes in the reasons why people chose the name they chose?
2. Which name seems to be the most favored? Why?
3. Which name is the least favored? Why?

Tell the group that all three names for this sacrament are equally appropriate. Each name highlights a different perspective on the same event. Distribute copies of the Sacrament Names section to three people and ask them to each read one of the sections.

After the sacrament names are read, discuss the following questions. Close the activity by either taking Communion together in a worship service or giving prayers of thanks for God's work in Jesus Christ.

Discussion Questions:

1. Which sacrament name or focus seems most like our church?
2. How does our church use all three focuses?
3. What should one consider when choosing a focus?
4. Which focus would be best for a Christmas Eve service? A service for Ash Wednesday? A Maundy Thursday service? An Easter service?
5. If you were designing a worship service for this group, which focus for the sacrament would you use?

Sacrament Names

The Lord's Supper: This name for Communion focuses on the reenactment of the supper Jesus had with the disciples on the night that he was betrayed and arrested. It highlights the confusion of the disciples, the melancholy mood of the meal, the sadness and fear of what might be to come, and the sense of a "good-bye" from Jesus.

The name denotes that the Communion table is the Lord's Table. God is the host. It is not just one congregation's meal. It is not just a Presbyterian meal. It is a table set by Jesus Christ for all who trust in him. We are reminded of Jesus' words on that very night to his disciples: "Do this in remembrance of me."

Communion: This name for Communion emphasizes the celebration of Communion. The meal celebrates that through Jesus' life, death, and resurrection, we are one with the risen Christ. We literally enact the symbol of taking Christ inside us. We recognize that we are part of Jesus Christ and he is part of us as individuals and as a church.

The name also celebrates our connection with one another. We are one community connected by Christ and communing together. Through Christ's sacrifice on the cross we are able to be reconnected with God and with one another. We are thankful that, through this meal, we are united with God's faithful people of every time and place.

The Eucharist: This name for Communion emphasizes "thanksgiving." The word *Eucharist* literally means "thanks." In this sacrament we give thanks to God for all God has done throughout the ages, particularly what God has done through the sacrifice of Jesus Christ.

The Eucharist usually takes place after the offering has been taken in a worship service. The bread and wine (or grape juice) are brought as an offering from the harvest of the earth. Within every Communion service in the PC(USA) and other Reformed denominations, we pray a great prayer of thanksgiving. It is often a long prayer because we have much for which we are thankful! In the Eucharist, we celebrate with thanksgiving the new and everlasting life that we receive through Jesus Christ.

2. Communion Name Pictures
(45 minutes, art)

Supplies: Three poster boards, markers, poster paints, brushes, other paint supplies, copies of the Sacrament Names sheet (on p. 112)

Directions: Gather your group together and introduce the topic of Communion by using the introduction from this chapter. This activity makes a great continuation of the previous activity. If you are starting with this activity, then read to the group the explanations for the three different names for Communion on the Sacrament Names sheet. Explain that although they all three refer to the same thing, the names reflect different perspectives on it.

Divide the group into three smaller groups. Give each small group a poster board, some markers or paints, and a copy of the Sacrament Names sheet. Then assign each group one of the names. Large youth groups may need to have more than three groups. Simply repeat the names between the small groups. It will be interesting to see the differences and commonalities between each group's results.

Ask each group to read again the information on its assigned sacrament name found on the Sacrament Names sheet. Then ask the youth to discuss the following questions:

1. What does this name tell us about the sacrament?
2. When we actually participate in Communion, how does this perspective become apparent?

After the small groups have read and discussed their name, invite them to work together to create a symbol or picture for the name and perspective that they were assigned.

After all the groups have finished, bring them back together in one large group. Ask each group to show its picture and ask the other groups to guess what name that group had. Next ask the group to explain its picture and how the picture communicates the word that group had. After each group shares, allow time for others to ask questions, make comments, and show their appreciation.

3. Communion Scramble
(20 minutes, game)

Supplies: Sheets of construction paper with the Communion elements (on p. 115) written on them, sheets of construction paper with the Communion element definitions written on them

Preparation: Using markers, write the Communion element names on paper (one name per paper). Then, write the definitions on another set of papers (one name per paper).

Directions: Gather the group and introduce the topic of Communion by using the introduction from this chapter. Ask the participants to close their eyes and picture a Communion service as they usually experience it. Slowly ask the following questions:

1. What are the different parts of Communion?
2. What happens first? Who does it?
3. What happens next?
4. Imagine the whole Communion service. What happens last?

After about three minutes of meditation, ask the participants to open their eyes.

Tell them that congregations sometimes differ in how they do Communion in terms of style and tone. However, a certain series of elements always occur and always take place in the same order.

Randomly place the Communion Element sheets in a vertical line on the floor. Randomly place the Communion Element Definition sheets to the right in a vertical line. Ask the group to work together to match the correct definition with the correct element name. Once the participants believe they have done this correctly, ask them to put the elements and their definitions in the correct chronological order. After the group believes it has completed the task correctly, check to see if everything is correct. Review each element and its definition. After each definition, make time for individuals to ask questions and make comments.

4. Breads of the World
(20–30 minutes, discussion)

Supplies: Something to drink (this activity will make participants thirsty), a variety of breads from different ethnic traditions. Examples: Italian bread, French bread, tortillas, pita bread, German rye, Korean rice cake, a cooked sweet potato (used in some places in Africa)

Preparation: Gather the breads from your local bakery or ask members of the church to bake several different kinds of bread.

Directions: Ask the participants to think about Communion services in which they have participated. Invite group members to share some of the services they have experienced. What do they remember most about them? Where were they? Who were they with? How did they actually receive the elements? What kind of bread did they use?

If your church is like many in our denomination, the bread used in Communion is either little cracker wafers or cubes of white bread. Explain to the group that no rule says we have to use any one kind of bread. Our Directory for Worship (basically the rule book for Presbyterian worship) found in the PC(USA)'s *Book of Order* simply states that we should use bread that is "common to the culture of the community" (W-3.3610). Communion is celebrated by Christians all over the world, and therefore, many kinds of bread are common.

Now show each bread you have collected, one at a time. Discuss what that bread is, where it comes from, and the culture that would commonly use the bread. Pass each bread around and invite participants to tear off a piece and try each one.

Communion Elements and Definitions

(listed chronologically)

Invitation: Calling the congregation to join in the feast that God has prepared.

Great thanksgiving: In prayer, the pastor and congregation praise God for God's gifts since creation, for Jesus Christ, and for the Holy Spirit's presence, which draws us together during this holy meal. The prayer concludes with the Lord's Prayer.

The words of institution: A recitation of 1 Corinthians 11:23–26 by the presiding minister.

Communion of the people: The presentation and distribution of the Communion elements.

Prayer after communion: A prayer thanking God for the gift of Communion and asking for God's grace and guidance in fulfilling our responsibilities as Christians.

Charge and blessing: The pastor gives direction to the congregation members about living their lives as Christians, and then gives God's blessing to the congregation.

This activity provides a great opportunity to have international missionaries or people in your congregation who have been on international mission trips to come and talk about their Communion experiences in different parts of the world. You may also ask people from different denominations to share their Communion experiences.

Close the activity with a prayer of thanksgiving for God's blessings of diversity and good food throughout the earth.

5. In Other Words
(30 minutes, discussion/writing)

Supplies: Pencils, paper, copies of the Communion Elements and Definitions sheet found in the Communion Scramble activity on page 115, copies of *The Book of Common Worship,* copies of your congregation's worship bulletin with the Communion liturgy in it

Preparation: Ask your pastor, youth director, or Christian educator to help you collect some copies of the PC(USA)'s *Book of Common Worship.* It is also on CD–ROM, and portions of it can be easily printed. You can also probably find copies in your presbytery's resource room. Ask your church secretary or clerk of session to help you find copies of a church bulletin with the Communion liturgy.

Directions: Introduce the topic of Communion by using the introduction from this chapter. This activity is an excellent follow-up to Communion Scramble.

Distribute the copies of the Communion Elements and Definitions sheet and your church bulletin. Briefly discuss the parts of a Communion service, including what they are and what purpose each part plays in the liturgy. Find where each element takes place in your church's Communion liturgy. Identify what your church does for each part.

Divide the groups into smaller groups of two to three people. Give each group copies of *The Book of Common Worship* (or the corresponding liturgy book of your denomination). Assign each group a part of the liturgy and tell the groups where they can find that liturgical element (see the list below).

Ask each group to read the liturgy aloud. If an element has more than one choice, read them all, and then ask the group to choose their favorite. Ask them to discuss what they believe the liturgy is trying to say. What does it mean? Why is it important?

Distribute the pens/pencils and paper. Ask the groups to rewrite the liturgy in their own words. When each group has finished, ask the groups to share their liturgy pieces in chronological order. After each group shares, make time for others to ask questions, make comments, and show their appreciation.

**Liturgical Elements of Communion
found in *The Book of Common Worship***

Invitation to the Lord's Table	pp. 68–69, 125
Great thanksgiving	pp. 69–73, 126–56, 165–400

6. Bringing in the Feast
(20–30 minutes, discussion)

Supplies: Newsprint, markers, tape

Directions: Gather the participants into a group and ask them to recall the way your congregation typically does a Communion service. Then, ask the following questions and record them on the newsprint:

1. Chronologically, how does Communion happen?
2. Who leads it?
3. What kind of bread and juice is used?
4. What kind of table service do you use (silver trays, pottery, etc.)?
5. What is the tone or mood during the service?

Next, ask the group members to recall any other Communion services they have attended (maybe at a conference, camp, youth retreat, or other special gathering). Repeat the questions and record the answers on the newsprint.

Now compare the different experiences of Communion. Discuss the following questions:

1. What is the same in all the Communion services?
2. What is different?

Explain to the group that some things will remain the same in all Presbyterian Communion services (or of your own tradition), but that the denomination also allows some discretion and flexibility in other ways. One aspect that can vary is the way the Communion elements themselves are brought into the room. Many place the elements on the table before the service begins, but others will bring them in at the beginning of the service in different ways. Ask the group members to brainstorm different ways that the Communion elements could be brought into the sanctuary at your church. Record their ideas on the newsprint.

Some examples are:

The bread and cup are carried up the center aisle during the first hymn.

The elements are brought from different parts of the sanctuary by people dressed in biblical period costumes.

Children and their parents could come out of the pews during the offering bringing grape juice and homemade bread.

On World Communion Sunday, people could enter the sanctuary dressed in international costumes bringing bread from their native culture.

After the group has brainstormed ideas, ask the youth to choose a few ideas that they think would be meaningful and realistic given the dynamics and abilities of their group or congregation. Share these ideas with your pastor and worship committee.

7. Communion Movie Clips
(1 hour, discussion)

Supplies: TV; VCR; movie clips that include scenes of the Lord's Supper, a symbolic allusion to Communion, or a significant, special, or holy meal; pens/pencils; paper; newsprint; markers

Preparation: Preview movies and choose the scenes you will show to the group. Some movies with communion scenes are *Babette's Feast, Jesus of Montreal, Jesus* (the network movie now on video), *Jesus of Nazareth, Godspell,* and *Jesus Christ Superstar.* Also, write the discussion questions on newsprint and post them on the wall.

Directions: Gather the group and introduce the topic of Communion by using the introduction from this chapter. Explain that you are going to show movie clips that portray scenes of the Lord's Supper, allusions to Communion, and/or other significant, special, or holy meals.

Distribute the pens/pencils and paper. Ask participants to write down the title of each movie as they see it and their impressions from each one. They can use the following questions to guide their answers.

Discussion Questions:

1. What is the director trying to communicate about the Last Supper?
2. How is the relationship between Jesus and his disciples portrayed?
3. What does the movie seem to be saying about us and our relationship with Jesus when we take Communion?

Give the title of each movie before showing each clip. After you have shown all the clips, discuss each clip by asking the participants to share their impressions, observations, and answers to the Discussion Questions. Record their answers on newsprint (one sheet of newsprint for each movie). Once you have discussed all the movie clips, ask the group the following questions:

1. How are the portrayals of the Last Supper similar?
2. How are they different?
3. Are there any themes that emerge?
4. What does all this say about God?
5. What does it say about us?
6. How has your perspective of Communion been changed, challenged, or affirmed?

8. Bread Making
(3–5 hours, including rising and baking time; art)

Supplies: A bread recipe, supplies and ingredients for making several loaves of bread (one loaf for every two to three people in your group)

Preparation: Place breadmaking supplies and ingredients in different places of the room or kitchen, allowing enough space for two to three people to work in each place. If you are an inexperienced cook or breadmaker, invite a few experienced cooks from your congregation to join the group.

Directions: Gather the group and introduce the topic of Communion by using the introduction from this chapter. Explain to the group members that they are going to be working together to make bread. Divide your group into smaller groups of two to three people. Tell the groups that it is important that they perform the steps of the breadmaking together and that you will be giving them the instructions to the recipe. Ask each group to move to a breadmaking station.

As you go through each step of making the bread, discuss the following questions with the group:

Adding the main ingredients of flour, sugar, salt, etc.

How is this mixture of different ingredients like our congregation?
How is it like the church worldwide?

Adding the yeast

How is the function of yeast in bread like the work of the Holy Spirit in you?
In the congregation?

Kneading the dough

How are we like the dough?
How are we like the hands that knead it?

Rising

How is the rising bread like our faith?
What does it take for the bread to rise?
What does it take for us to grow in faith?

Punching the dough

What are some times when you have felt "punched down"?
What is the function of punching down dough in making bread? What is it in our lives?

Baking

When are the times in life when you have "gone through some heat"?
What have been "heated times" for our group or congregation?
How do these times refine us and bring about a better result than a "gooey" or "sticky" one?

While the bread is rising and then baking, the group could do a service project, play games, study other aspects of worship in this book, worship together, or do a Bible study. You will have plenty of time to do some activities.

When the bread is done, gather the group and have a "popcorn" style prayer, offering to God thoughts and reflections from your conversations. There are several options for using the bread: give the bread to a local soup kitchen, eat the bread as a meal with grape juice as the drink, use the bread at an upcoming Communion service with your congregation, or take the loaves of bread to homebound members of your congregation.

9. Last Supper Meditation
(30 minutes, discussion)

Supplies: Bible

Directions: Gather the participants into a group and explain to them that they will be experiencing a guided meditation on the Last Supper. Explain that each person will be assigned a character. Everyone should go through the meditation thinking from the perspective of his or her character. The participants are to pay special attention to what is said to their character and to what their character says to others. The characters are Judas, Peter, Jesus, and the other disciples. As you lead the meditation, speak very slowly. Allow plenty of time for the participants to visualize the story and also meditate on it.

Ask the participants to find a comfortable position to lie or sit in and then close their eyes. Ask them, beginning with their head and neck muscles, to go down their body slowly, tightening and then releasing and relaxing each part of their body. You, as the leader, should guide them in this process by naming the body parts in order: head, neck, shoulders, chest, arms, fingers, hips, legs, feet, and toes.

Continue the meditation by saying the following: "Picture yourself in the upper room. Jesus and the disciples are all there. You have just finished the Passover meal. Imagine what you are wearing, the sights around the room, the smells of food and drink. You look around the table and see the people who have become your family, your life."

Read Matthew 26:20–35 (preferably in an easily understood translation such as NRSV or NIV). When you finish reading the Scripture, continue by saying, "Now separate yourself from this scene. Raise your consciousness above it and see it below you as you pull away and move into the present, here in this room with your friends. Open your eyes."

Gather the group together and ask the youth to discuss their experience from their character's perspective. Use the following questions for discussion:

1. What were you feeling during the meditation?
2. What were you thinking?
3. What was your motivation for being there? For your actions?
4. What did you think about the others around you?
5. What is important to you?

Then ask the group members to discuss the following questions from their own perspective:

1. With which character do you have the most in common?
2. Which character is most different from you?
3. What is your motivation for participating in Communion?
4. What realizations or thoughts do you have about Communion?

Close the activity by sharing a prayer of thanksgiving for Jesus' life, death, and resurrection, which we remember and celebrate through Communion.

CHAPTER 13

Baptism

Baptism is one of two sacraments recognized in the PC(USA) and many other Protestant denominations. Baptism is a symbol of being incorporated into (or being made a part of) Jesus Christ (*Book of Order* W-2.3001). Not that we become Christ, but we are made a part of the body of Christ, God's family. When Jesus was baptized, his identity was revealed as he was anointed by the Holy Spirit and proclaimed to be God's holy and beloved Son. In the same way, when we are baptized, God claims us and gives us an identity as God's child.

It is through Jesus' death and resurrection that God claims us as a part of God's family. Baptism is the symbol of this claim. We use water as the metaphorical symbol for the experience of death and resurrection through Jesus Christ. When individuals go under the water, they die to what separates them from God. When they come out from the water, they are raised to a new life with Christ.

The Presbyterian Church (U.S.A.) and many other Protestant denominations recognize both infant and adult baptism. In infant baptism, parents bring their baby before the congregation. The parents make a public profession of faith and promise to live the Christian faith and teach that faith to their child. The congregation promises to guide and nurture the baby in faith, as well as encourage the child to be a faithful member of the church (*Book of Common Worship,* p. 406). The minister then prays over the water and for the baptism. Typically in a Presbyterian service, the baby is then sprinkled with water as the minister says, "I baptize you in the name of the Father, and of the Son, and of the Holy Spirit" (*Book of Common Worship,* p. 413). At this point, many ministers carry the baby into the congregation where the infant is introduced as the newest member in the family of God.

In an adult baptism, the adult makes a public profession of faith. Prayers are said over the water and for the baptism. Then, the person is baptized. After the baptism, the minister welcomes the individual into the family of God on behalf of the congregation. Many times the person is asked to remain after the service so that others may greet him or her personally.

When we are baptized, we begin our life in Christ. Whether our baptism occurs when we were infants or by our own choosing as adults, it witnesses to the same truth. God establishes a covenant relationship with us. It is our responsibility to maintain this relationship throughout our Christian life.

Every time we witness a baptism, we have the opportunity to be reminded of our own baptism and recommit ourselves to God's faithful, grace-filled presence in our lives. A baptism is an opportunity for us to reaffirm our own baptism. During a baptism, we hear the same vows that parents, congregations, or we ourselves made during our own baptism. We also make vows to infants and their parents as we promise to guide and nurture a child in the faith. In hearing those vows, we hear our own calling to live as a disciple of Christ (*Book of Order* W-2.3002). These promises command us to go and teach others the faith so that they might know God's grace and mercy in their lives. In baptism, the community is bound together and renewed in its commitment to be the body of Christ in the world (Stookey 1982).

Baptism, like Communion, is most appropriately celebrated after the hearing and proclamation of the Word, because a sacrament is an enactment of God's Word. We respond to God's Word by acting upon it. Baptism is a sign of God's promise of faithfulness to the people and should come after the people have heard the Word (God's promises) proclaimed.

The following activities are designed to teach the basic elements of baptism, engage young people in the many dimensions of baptism, and enable them to experience the sacrament in new ways. People who are preparing to make a public profession of faith (for example, a confirmation class) may find it beneficial to explore the purpose and nature of baptism through these activities. A clearer understanding of baptism can lead to insight as one writes a personal statement of faith. See chapter 7 for further insight on writing a faith statement.

The majority of these activities assume that the people participating in them have been baptized. However, this may or may not be the case with your group. Check with your group members or their parents before proceeding and adapt the activities as needed.

ACTIVITIES

1. Reaffirmation of Baptismal Covenant
(50 minutes, discussion)

Supplies: Copies of the liturgy for one of the services for a reaffirmation of the baptismal covenant (found on pp. 431–88 of *The Book of Common Worship*), pens/pencils, paper, newsprint

Preparation: Choose one of the services of reaffirmation. Choose and/or reserve a worship space. You may do this anywhere (outside, in your sanctuary, on the beach, etc.). Make arrangements for your minister to attend this session and lead the reaffirmation service. You may also want to arrange for someone to lead a few songs during the reaffirmation service.

Directions: Distribute a copy of the reaffirmation service to everyone in your group, along with pens/pencils and paper. Ask the participants to find a partner and read through the service together. Ask them to discuss the following questions:

1. What is the emphasis of the service?
2. What is the service's significance?
3. Why do something like this?
4. What is the service asking people to say?

Tell them to write down any responses or further questions they have about the service.

Gather the group together and list the questions and responses on a piece of newsprint. Allow time for the group to make comments about the responses and discuss the questions listed. Next, invite the group to move to the worship space and participate in the service.

Discussion Questions: After you have finished, use the following questions to examine the experience. Remember to help participants speak more in specifics than in generalities. You may meet in small groups or as one large group, depending on the size and dynamics of your group. If you meet in small groups, ask the youth to come back together and share the highlights of their discussions. Allow time for others to make comments and/or ask questions.

1. What were you thinking or feeling during the service?
2. What was most significant for you and why?
3. What words stood out for you?
4. How did this service develop or change your understanding of baptism or your relationship with God?

2. Remembering Your Baptism
(45 minutes, discussion)

Supplies: TV/VCR, pens/pencils and paper

Preparation: In this age of video cameras and digital imagery, it is likely that several participants have a videotape of their baptism. Ask the participants to bring their videos to this session. Make sure you ask them to have the tape set to the baptismal service itself. This will save time during the activity. Also, ask all participants to find out what they can about their own baptisms from their parents, guardians, or grandparents.

Directions: View the baptism videos that the participants have brought. Afterwards, ask all the participants to share stories of their own baptism. Discuss the following questions: What is similar about the baptisms? What is different?

Next, distribute pens/pencils and paper to the participants. Invite them to write their baptismal story. The story can be a retelling of what happened, it can be a reflection on baptism (from their personal experience or as a general statement), or it could take the form of a poem, prayer, or song. Tell the youth they can be as creative as they want to be as long as they stay on task. Give them fifteen minutes to write.

Gather the group together and invite the participants to share their baptismal stories. Allow time for people to make comments, ask questions, and show their appreciation.

If the group chooses to do so, put the stories in a notebook and keep them in a special place (such as the youth room). You may add to the baptism book as time goes on. If you perform a service for renewal, you could ask the participants to write about that experience and put it in the notebook. Use the notebook to read stories of faith as young people struggle to grow and develop their own faith.

3. Water Meditation
(30 minutes, meditation)

Supplies: Chime or bell, a recording of water sounds, a small fountain, or a large bowl of water and pitcher of water (or go outside to a stream, river, lake, or other body of water)

Preparation: Collect the different sounds of water listed above and put them in the place where you will be meeting, or make arrangements to go to a place with water. Also, choose from among these references a few Scripture passages for meditation:

Baptism Scripture Passages

Genesis 17:7–8	The faithfulness of God
Acts 22:14–16	Call to baptism
Titus 3:5–8	God's act of forgiveness
Matthew 3:13–17,	Jesus' baptism
1 Corinthians 12:12–31	Baptism makes us one body of Christ
Romans 6:3–11, Ephesians 5:14	New life in Christ through baptism
Ephesians 4:4–6	One baptism in Christ
Galatians 3:27, 28	One in Christ
1 Peter 2:9	God's chosen people
Romans 6:3, 4	Death and resurrection through Christ
Matthew 28:18–20	The Great Commissioning
Acts 2:37–42	The huge baptism after Pentecost

Directions: Ask the participants to sit in a comfortable position. Explain to them that a meditation is a time of relaxed concentration on a certain theme. Today, you are giving them the opportunity to meditate on baptism.

Ask the participants to take in five or six slow, deep breaths (breathe in for five counts, breathe out for five counts). Next, draw their attention to the sound of the water (recorded or real). Ask them to quiet their minds and focus solely on the sound of the water.

Then, tell the youth that you are going to read several Scripture passages. Tell them that they will know when you are going to the next Scripture passage when they hear the ringing of the bell or chime. Ask them to picture themselves in the passage. What are they thinking? What do they feel? What are they doing? How do they react?

Begin reading Scripture. Read slowly, allowing for a time of silence between each verse. When you finish reading the Scripture passages, ask the youth to focus solely on the sound of the water. Give them time to listen to the water, and then ring the chime and ask them to take in a few more deep breaths. Ask them to turn their thoughts toward God in prayer. After a few more minutes, ring the chime again, say "Amen," and ask the participants to open their eyes when they want to.

Discussion Questions: After the meditation, discuss the following questions. Remember to help participants speak more in specifics than in generalities. You may meet in small groups or as one large group, depending on the size and dynamics of your group. If you meet in small groups, ask the youth to come together and share the highlights of their discussions. Allow time for others to make comments and/or ask questions.

1. What were you thinking or feeling during the meditation?
2. What images did you see or think about?
3. What roles did Jesus play?
4. When you imagined yourself in the scene with Jesus speaking to you, how did you react? What were you feeling and thinking?
5. What new questions do you have?
6. How has your idea of baptism been challenged, changed, or expanded through this activity?

4. Water Tour of the Bible
(20 minutes, drama/writing/discussion)

Supplies: Bibles, Scripture references, paper, pens/pencils, newsprint, markers

Preparation: Review the Scripture references found below and choose as many as you need for your group.

Water Scripture Passages

Genesis 1:1–8	Creation
Genesis 7–8:22	Noah and the flood
Exodus 2:1–10	Baby Moses in the river
Exodus 14:21–31	Crossing the Red Sea
Numbers 20:1–13	Moses strikes the rock
Psalms 18:16–19; 69:1–3, 13–15; 144:7–8	Water images
Isaiah 12:3–4	Water of salvation

Isaiah 43:1–3a	God's presence in the waters
Isaiah 44:3–4	Waters for the thirsty land
Ezekiel 36:25–28	Renewal of Israel
Amos 5:24	Justice rolls down like water
Matthew 3:11–12	John the Baptist
Matthew 3:13–17	Jesus' baptism
John 4:7–15	Woman at the well/living water
John 7:37–38	Living Water
1 Peter 3:18–22	Saved through water of baptism

Directions: Divide your group into smaller groups of three or four people. Distribute Bibles and assign each group one of the water Scripture passages. Ask the participants to read their passage. Invite each group to tell the story of its passage. Encourage the youth to be creative by using or creating a song, a skit, or a liturgical movement. For instance, the Noah's Ark passage could incorporate singing "Row, Row, Row Your Boat."

Gather the groups together and ask them to share their stories. Allow time after each group's presentation for others to guess what water story the group is portraying, to ask questions, to make comments, and to show their appreciation. Then, ask the youth to return to their small groups. Invite the small groups to write a prayer thanking God for what God did in their Bible passage. They may write a poem, put movements to a prayer, or write a song.

Gather the groups together and ask them to share their prayers.

5. Turning Away from Evil
(30 minutes, discussion)

Supplies: Newsprint, markers, *The Book of Common Worship*

Directions: Gather the youth into a group and ask them to brainstorm things that interfere with their relationship with God. Ask them to be specific. Write their answers on the newsprint. Next, ask them to identify categories within the list they brainstormed. In other words, their ideas might fall under the categories of peer pressure, money, people, food, and so forth. Discuss the following questions:

1. What things seem to be commonly the hardest to deal with?
2. Which ones seem more like bad habits that could possibly be simple to break?
3. How do these things cause problems with your faith?
4. How do these actions make you feel secure?
5. How do they make you anxious? (How do they bother you?)
6. What can you do to change your actions or relieve your anxiety?

Next, read the Profession of Faith statement and questions found in *The Book of Common Worship* on pages 406–08. Discuss the following question: What does our baptism call us to be and to do?

Next, divide your group into smaller groups of three or four people. Distribute newsprint and markers and ask each group to write a prayer for guidance and help to turn away from evil. Gather together again and ask the groups to share their prayers.

6. Blue Cloth
(30–45 minutes, liturgical movement)

Supplies: Recording of water sounds, large strips of lightweight blue cloth (two feet by six to eight feet). Look for satin, chiffon, lamai, light cotton, etc.

Preparation: Arrange to meet in a place that has plenty of room to move around and use the cloth like parachutes.

Directions: The group will use the cloth as a symbol of the waters of baptism or being clothed as a new creation. You may want to do this with the meditation or reaffirmation of baptismal vows.

Divide your group into pairs. The pairs should hold a piece of blue cloth between them. Ask the participants to experiment with ways they can move with the cloth. Encourage them to make this time playful and creative. Tell them there is no right or wrong way to move the cloth. Ask them to move the cloth slowly, then fast. Up, then down. In circles, then whipping it around in straight lines. Now ask them to imagine that the cloth is water. Ask them to make the cloth look like a wave, a waterfall, a waterspout, a geyser, a lake, a stream or river, and a rain shower. Ask them to move the cloth to recorded water sounds. Invite them to move around the room while keeping the cloth in motion.

Next ask the group to stand in one big circle while still holding the cloth. Ask the whole group to make the cloth look like an ocean, a lake, and a river. While leaving the cloth in the shape of a river, a few participants should pick it up and hold it about waist-high so that others may walk into the river. They will need to hold up the cloth during the meditation time that follows. Other participants will need to take over holding the cloth so that all have a chance to walk into the water.

Tell the group that you are now going to shift the activity into a time of prayer and meditation. Play some quiet music (either water sounds or instrumental music). Ask the participants to close their eyes and imagine what it feels like to be washed clean from sin. Ask them to imagine what it feels like to jump into a river or pool. Ask them to imagine what it feels like when you get out and the wind hits your clean skin.

Invite small groups of people to enter the river, stay for a while, and then slowly leave while you read Scripture or baptismal liturgy. Tell them to sit quietly by the water's edge after they are done. Find the baptismal liturgy in *The Book of Common Worship* (pp. 403–88). You may choose Scripture from the readings cited in the Water Meditation activity.

After everyone has walked through the water, put the river back on the floor. While the youth are still seated around the water, use the questions below to discuss their experience.

Discussion Questions:

1. What did we do with the blue cloth? Start from the beginning and recount every-thing you did (from being in partners, to the whole group, to the meditation).
2. What were you thinking or feeling as you played with the cloth?
3. What was fun about playing with the cloth?
4. What was embarrassing about playing with the cloth?
5. When you were in the water, what did you think about?
6. When you were in the water, what did you feel?
7. Did you want to stay in the water or hurry up and get out?
8. How has this activity added to your understanding of baptism?

7. A New Name
(20–30 minutes, discussion/writing)

Supplies: Paper, pens/pencils, markers, baby-name books

Directions: Distribute the pens/pencils and paper. Ask the group members to write their name in big bold letters at the top of the paper. Then, ask them to think of fif-teen ways to answer the question "Who are you?" In responding to this question, they should think not only about their roles (daughter, sister, etc.) but also about their gifts, their talents, and who God is intending them to be. Some people will have trouble writing positive things about themselves, so tell the participants to pre-tend they are being paid $10,000 for every answer they put down. As the partici-pants are writing, pass around a few baby-name books and invite the participants to include the meaning of their name on the list.

After everyone has finished, divide the group into smaller groups of two or three people. Ask the participants to share their lists in their groups. If a participant has not written down fifteen items, ask the others in the group to add to that per-son's list.

Gather the groups together. Tell them that, historically, Native Americans were often named for traits that they were perceived to have, that their parents had, or that they hoped to have in the future. Ask the group to call out some familiar fic-tional or nonfictional Native American names (Sitting Bull, Crazy Horse, Bear Foot, Kicking Bird, Stands With A Fist, Dances With Wolves, Flying Eagle). Ask them to brainstorm why these names would be given to someone.

Now ask the participants to turn their papers over and write in big bold letters a Native American name for themselves that reflects the characteristics they wrote for themselves on the other side. Invite participants to share their names. Close in a prayer thanking God for the gift of our identity.

8. Average vs. Baptized
(30–45 minutes, art/discussion)

Supplies: Newsprint, markers, tape

Directions: Gather your group and divide them into smaller groups of four people. Distribute markers and newsprint. Ask each group to draw an average young person of today. Encourage the group to think about themselves, the youth at school, and the youth in their community. They should draw the picture with little lines coming out from the person where they can describe the item on that person. For example, they may draw a youth with a pierced nose and have a line going to the description "latest must-have body piercing." Encourage them to think not only about what the young person would look like but what the person might be carrying or have with him or her that represents that person's interests (church, sports, friends, etc.).

Gather the groups together and have a spokesperson from each group "introduce" that group's "youth." Allow time for others to ask questions, make comments, and show their appreciation. Next, ask the participants to return to their smaller groups. Ask them to add to their drawing by now thinking of their person as being baptized. Ask them to think about what it means to be a baptized member of the family of God. How does it change their perspective? Their behavior? Who they hang around with? For example, they might add a line coming from a smile: "Can find hope in the good times and the bad."

Invite the groups to share their drawings again and talk about how their young person changed when they were baptized and became a member of the family of God. Tape the "youth" on the walls. Then, ask the participants to share specific real-life ways that being a Christian has made a difference in their personal lives. Encourage them to be specific.

9. Family Rituals
(30 minutes, discussion)

Supplies: Newsprint, markers, pens/pencils, paper, tape

Directions: Ask the participants to brainstorm yearly holidays, events, or rituals that are important to their family (Christmas, birthdays, summer vacations, game nights, Thanksgiving, etc.). Write the events on the newsprint.

Next, distribute the pens/pencils and paper. Ask each participant to pick out one thing from the list and write in detail who is usually there, what kind of meals are served, what conversations take place, what the family does together, what rituals or traditions take place, and where it occurs. Ask the participants to come back to the whole group and share why they like the rituals they chose to write about. Write their answers on the newsprint.

Sometimes talking about family rituals can be painful because of negative dynamics in a family or the absence of family members through death or divorce. Keep this in mind as you do this activity and be sensitive to young people's ability to participate in the conversation. Let them participate at their own level in their own way.

Next, ask the youth to brainstorm a list of celebrations or rituals of the church (such as Communion, baptism, youth Sunday, Maundy Thursday service, or candlelight services). Ask them to pick their favorite one and tell why it is their favorite. Write their reasons on another sheet of newsprint.

Now ask the participants to compare the church rituals with the family rituals. Discuss the following: What makes the rituals different? What do they have in common? What makes religious rituals important? What makes family rituals important?

Explain that baptism is one of the most important rituals of the church. Use the introduction to this chapter to further your explanation. Now discuss the following: What is significant about the baptism ritual? Does the church have ways it ensures that the promises made by the congregation during baptism are fulfilled throughout a persons' life?

Finally, ask the youth to brainstorm rituals they could create to remind them of the promises of baptism (sharing faith stories, formally thanking their Sunday school teachers or youth advisors, etc.). Ask the group members to choose one activity on their list to do.

10. Jesus' Baptism
(30 minutes, drama)

Supplies: Bibles or copies of the Gospel stories

Preparation: Prepare a copy of the four Gospel texts of Jesus' baptism. They are Matthew 3:13–17; Mark 1:9–11; Luke 3:21–23; and John 1:19–34.

Directions: Divide your group into smaller groups of three to five people. Assign each group one of the four texts. Ask the groups to read their text. Next, invite them to divide up the parts in their text and practice acting out their passage. They may do it silently with one person reading, or they can do it in a dialogue. Encourage them to be as creative as they want.

After everyone is ready, ask each group to present its version to the whole group. Discuss the following:

1. What are the differences and similarities between the passages?
2. What is the significance of the differences?
3. How do the differences highlight one part of the story over another?
4. What is the announcement that the dove or Holy Spirit makes?
5. To whom is the announcement made (Jesus or the crowd)?

After the discussion, explain that in his baptism, Jesus is identified as God' Son. In our baptism, we too are given our identity as God's child. Ask the participants to find a partner. Ask them to stand facing each other and repeat after you the following:

> _____ (name)
> You are a child of God.
> God loves you.
> God is well pleased with you.
> You are God's delight!*
> Amen.
>
> *The alternate meaning in Greek for "well pleased" is "delight."*

11. Baptism Mosaic
(30 minutes, art)

Supplies: Scraps of different shades of blue paper, plus other collage materials that can symbolize water (paint, foil, cloth, etc.), glue, scissors, large piece of newsprint or butcher paper for the banner

Preparation: Cut the paper and other materials into small pieces. They do not have to be perfect squares but should be about two inches by two inches in size.

Directions: Give each person in your group a handful of blue pieces of paper. On the darkest shades of paper, ask the participants to write who they are (youth, child of God, singer, dancer, actor, good listener, friend, etc.). Encourage them to include not only their roles in life but also their gifts and talents. On the medium shades, ask them to write God's blessings in their lives (courage, peace, confidence, help through a difficult time, etc.). On the lightest shades of paper, ask them to write characteristics of God (Holy, Creator, faithful, protector, etc.). When the participants have finished, ask them to share in small groups what they wrote on their pieces of paper.

Gather the group and invite the youth to work together to design and make a mosaic that symbolizes baptism by using their pieces of paper and the other supplies provided. Some options are to make a cross, a dove, a river, or a path. Encourage them to be as creative as they want.

12. Bead Bracelet
(25 minutes, art/discussion)

Supplies: Several colors of beads, leather string or yarn

Preparation: Collect purple, white, green, black, yellow, red, and blue beads. Divide the beads into separate colors. Cut leather or yarn into twelve-inch lengths.

Directions: Give each person in your group a piece of leather or yarn and ask the youth to sit in a circle. Place the beads in the middle of the circle so that everyone can reach them. Distribute Bibles to seven volunteers and assign each of them one of the following Bible verses:

1. Genesis 17:7–8: The faithfulness of God (purple—God's sovereignty)
2. Matthew 3:13–17: Jesus' baptism (white—Jesus' holiness)
3. Acts 22:14–16: The call to baptism (green—means go!)
4. 1 Corinthians 12:12–31: Baptism makes us one in Christ (black—all the colors into one)
5. Romans 6:3–11, Ephesians 5:14: New life in Christ through baptism (yellow—the sunshine of a new day)
6. Romans 6:3–4: Death and resurrection through Christ (red—Jesus' blood shed for us)
7. 1 Peter 2:9: We are God's chosen people (blue for the waters of baptism)

Tell the participants that they are going to make a bead bracelet (or a necklace, choker, or ankle bracelet) that represents baptism. Each bead will symbolize a certain aspect of baptism identified in the Scripture reading. After each Scripture reading, invite the group to choose the appropriate bead and discuss the following questions:

1. What does this Scripture mean to us?
2. What difference does it make in our lives?
3. What does it say about God? About Jesus?
4. What does it say about baptism?

In closure, remind the groups about the purpose of their bracelets. They symbolize God's permanent claim on us as God's children and the joy, grace, and hope in being a child of God.

WORKS CITED

Book of Order. 2000. Louisville, Ky.: The Office of the General Assembly.

Stookey, Laurence Hull. *Baptism: Christ's Act in the Church.* 1982. Nashville: Abingdon Press.

The Theology and Worship Ministry Unit, *Book of Common Worship.* 1993. Louisville, Ky.: Westminster/John Knox Press.